Korean
phrasebook

Kim, Young Ok
Robert Joseph Dowling

Korean Phrasebook
2nd edition

Published by
   Lonely Planet Publications
   Head Office: PO Box 617, Hawthorn, Vic 3122, Australia
   Branches: 150 Linden St, Oakland, CA 94607, USA
                  10a Spring Place, London NW5 3BH, UK
                  1 rue du Dahomey, 75011 Paris, France

Printed by
   Colorcraft Ltd, Hong Kong
   Printed in China

This edition was written by Kim, Young Ok and Robert Dowling. Louise Callan edited the book and Rachel Black was responsible for design and illustrations. The cover was designed by Valerie Tellini. For their forbearance, the authors would like to thank their children, Nerida and Matthew. Thanks also to Yim, Doo Hyuk in Korea and Shin, Ki Hyun in Canberra for their assistance.

Published
   June 1995

Cover Photo
   Painting on Pori-sa Temple. Photograph by Martin Moos.

National Library of Australia Cataloguing in Publication Data

Dowling, Kim Young Ok
   Korean Phrasebook.
   2nd ed.
   ISBN 0 86442 302 0

   1. Korean Language - Conversation and phrase books - English. I. Chambers, Kevin. Korean phrasebook. II Title. III. Title: Korean phrasebook.
   (Series: Lonely Planet language survival kit).

495.783421

Contents

Introduction

Confucius

Korea has a rich cultural heritage. The evolution of Korean culture has been influenced by periods of instability and violent interaction with the Mongols and various Chinese and Japanese dynasties, and by periods of stability and isolation. Within this climate, uniquely Korean traditions were established and developed in the areas of literature, art, music, education, government and social values and structures. Religious and philosophical influences have been important in this evolutionary process – specifically shamanism, Confucianism, Buddhism and, more recently, Christianity.

The Korean language has also evolved. Although it is classified as a member of the Altaic family, which includes Manchu, Mongolian and Turkish, no-one knows for certain how long it has been spoken. Despite the geographical proximity of the countries, Korean is quite unlike Chinese and Japanese.

Chinese characters were used to write Korean until the 15th century. However, as they were difficult to learn and were quite different from the Korean spoken language, most people remained illiterate. In 1446, after many years of study and testing by the ruler at the time, King Sejong, and his scholars, a unique

7

Korean alphabet, *hunminjŏngŭm*, was introduced. It was devised on a purely phonetic basis and consisted of 28 letters. These were arranged in syllable units or blocks and not into linear words. This meant that the syllables could be written horizontally or vertically on a page. *Hunminjŏngŭm* has evolved into the modern Korean alphabet, *hangŭl*, which has 24 letters and follows the Western convention of writing from left to right across a page. Although some Chinese characters are still used today in conjunction with the Korean alphabet, especially in newspapers, high-level communication in Korean is possible without using them. Therefore, they are not included in this book.

Today, Korean is spoken by nearly 67 million people, of which about 63 million live on the Korean peninsula and islands, and the remaining four million abroad. It is the official language of North and South Korea and is used in education and all cultural and business activities.

There are six main dialects on the Korean peninsula and one on Cheju Island. The dialect spoken in and around Seoul is referred to as Standard Korean. As travel to and within North Korea is still very restricted, this phrasebook uses Standard Korean and is mainly directed towards people travelling within South Korea. In the major cities, you will usually be able to find someone who speaks some English.

There are two forms of speech in everyday use. Formal/polite expressions are used with people who are your senior in age or position, and informal/casual expressions are used with friends, family and close associates or people who are your junior in age or position. Unless indicated, we have used formal/polite expressions throughout this book.

In 1986, the Department of Education (South Korea) published the *Approved Korean Spelling of Foreign Words* and, in 1988, the

Revised Korean Spelling and Pronunciation System of Korean.
These have been followed in this phrasebook.

Any attempt by you to speak Korean will be well received, and
as you move out from the cities, this book will provide invaluable
help as you interact with the Korean people. Also of help are
Lonely Planet's guides to *Korea* and *Seoul*.

We wish you well in your travels.
jŭl-kŏ-un yŏ-haeng-i doe-shi-   즐거운 여행이 되시기를!
ki-rŭl!

Abbreviations Used in This Book
adj - adjective
adv - adverb
f - feminine
inf - informal
lit - literally
m - masculine
n - noun
v - verb

Help!

There are some essential words you should know in any language.
Try to memorise these to make your stay a little smoother. `Yes'
is 예 *(ye)* and `no' is 아니오 *(a-ni-o)* but check page 23 before
replying to a question or you may find yourself in a confusing
situation. Koreans do not use the word `please' as we do in
English. However, when using the polite form to request something, Koreans say 'Please give me...', 주십시오(*ju-ship-shi-yo*).
`Thank you' is 감사합니다 (*kam-sa-ham-ni-da*). Page 30 will
give you details on how to greet Koreans correctly but you can't

10 Help!

go wrong if you use 안녕하십니까 (*an-nyŏng-ha-shim-ni-kka*) as a general `hello' and 안녕히 가십시오 (*an-nyŏng-hi ka-ship-shi-yo*) for `goodbye'. If you want to make small talk, look on page 40 for some easy phrases. Page 47 will get you out of trouble if you haven't understood something.

Pronunciation

The modern Korean alphabet, *hangŭl*, has 24 letters – 10 vowels and 14 consonants. Korean has an additional 11 vowel sounds, produced by combining two of the basic 10 vowels and five double consonants. This results in 40 distinctive basic sounds. There are also 11 complex consonant combinations.

Romanisation

A Romanised version of the *hangŭl* letters is used in this book. This Romanisation is loosely based on the system used by the Korean Government which is based on the McCune-Reischauer (M-R) System. As Korean has a phonetic alphabet, it is easiest to learn the language by making the effort to learn the correct pronunciation of each of the Korean vowels and consonants as listed in this chapter. However, Korean does have some sounds not found in English and it is important to remember that Romanisation of these only provides an approximation of Korean pronunciation.

Although your own pronunciation will be understood by most Koreans, accurate pronunciation will only be achieved by listening to and imitating native Korean speakers.

With the exception of the Grammar chapter, each English phrase in this book is accompanied by both the Korean script and its Romanisation.

Let's go!   *kap-shi-da!*   갑시다 !

Vowels

a	as in sh**ah**	ㅏ
ya	as in **y**ard	ㅑ
ŏ	as in **a**gree	ㅓ
yŏ	as in **o**nion	ㅕ
o	as in r**aw**	ㅗ
yo	as in **yo**re	ㅛ
u	as in w**oo**	ㅜ
yu	as in **you**	ㅠ
ŭ	as in brok**e**n	ㅡ
i	as in **i**nn	ㅣ

Vowel Combinations

ae	as in **a**pple	ㅐ
yae	as in **ye**t	ㅒ
e	as in n**e**t	ㅔ
ye	as in **ye**ah	ㅖ
oe	as in w**ay**	ㅚ
wi	as in **we**	ㅟ
ŭi	as in sq**uee**ze	ㅢ
wa	as in **wa**nder	ㅘ
wae	as in **wa**g	ㅙ
wŏ	as in **wo**rry	ㅝ
we	as in **we**dding	ㅞ

Consonants

Korean consonants are pronounced with various degrees of aspiration (pronunciation of a letter with a puff of unvoiced air, eg `p' in party) and glottalisation (short, sharp sound made at the back of the throat, eg the cockney sound of `tt' in butter). The middle position of a word occurs where one consonant ends a syllable and another consonant begins the next. When a syllable ending in a consonant is followed by a syllable beginning with a vowel, the consonant is often pronounced as the first letter of the following syllable. An apostrophe after a letter indicates that it is aspirated and should, therefore, be pronounced with extra breath.

Single

Korean	Romanisation		
Letter	*Initial*	*Middle*	*Final*
ㄱ	k	g	k
ㄴ	n	n	n
	–	l (when followed by ㄹ)	
ㄷ	d	d	t
ㄹ	r	l	l
ㅁ	m	m	m
ㅂ	b	m	p
ㅅ	s	s	t
	sh (when followed by ㅣ)	–	
ㅇ	–	ng	ng
ㅈ	j	ch	t
ㅊ	ch'	ch'	t
ㅋ	k'	k'	k
ㅌ	t'	t'	t
ㅍ	p'	p'	p
ㅎ	h	h	–

Double

ㄲ	kk	g	k
ㄸ	tt	–	–
ㅃ	pp	–	–
ㅆ	s	ss	d
ㅉ	jj	–	–

Complex

These are never in the initial-syllable position.

Korean		Romanisation		
Letter	*Initial*	*Middle*	*Final*	*Example*
ㄳ	–	g	k	넋
ㄵ	–	nj	n	앉다
ㄶ	–	nh	n	많다
ㄺ	–	lg	g	읽다
ㄻ	–	lm	m	삶다
ㄼ	–	lb	b	얇다
ㄽ	–	ls	l	외곬
ㄾ	–	lt	l	핥다
ㄿ	–	lp	b	읊다
ㅀ	–	rr	l	싫다
ㅄ	–	bs	b	값

Syllable Structure

Korean words are constructed of blocks of syllables with letters positioned according to prescribed rules dating from the 15th century. Each syllable must have at least one vowel, and every written syllable must begin with a consonant.

Stress

Generally, words and syllables are given equal stress when speaking Korean. However, glottalised and aspirated consonants are given distinctive stress.

Grammar

Apart from the adoption of a selection of Chinese words and characters, the Korean language expresses a unique cultural heritage of more than two thousand years. It reflects the way Koreans think, reason and live. As a consequence of Korean remaining relatively untouched by the influence of other languages, its structure is quite different from that of most Western languages. It is important to remember, therefore, that simple translation of a Korean phrase into a common English phrase would sometimes fail to communicate its cultural significance.

Sentence Structure
The basic word order of a Korean sentence is subject-object-verb. The verb always comes last in a sentence, and subordinate clauses always precede the main clause. `I like Korean food' would read as `I Korean food like' in Korean. However, the subject and object word order can be changed (object-subject-verb) for emphasis.

Koreans usually omit any details from a sentence that are obvious from the context. The subject is often omitted in spoken Korean, so the sentence would be reduced to `Korean food like'.

Be aware that Koreans may sometimes omit the subject of a sentence when they are speaking English, making understanding difficult.

Nouns
Korean nouns do not have articles, gender or plural forms. The word *shin-mun* can mean `newspaper', `a newspaper', `the newspaper', `some newspapers' or `the newspapers'.

15

GRAMMAR

Classifiers

Classifiers, or counting units, are used in Korean to indicate the nature of various objects being counted. For example, in `three cartons of milk', `cartons' is the classifier. They are also used to express the plural when necessary. They usually follow nouns and numerals. The classifier, *-kae*, is used when there is no other specific classifier for a particular item:

- For inanimate objects: *kae*

ŭi-ja du kae	two chairs
(lit: chair two *kae*)	
ch' aek-sang ne kae	four desks
(lit: desk four *kae*)	

- For animals: *ma-ri*

so se ma-ri	three cows
(lit: cow three *ma-ri*)	
mal da-sŏt ma-ri	five horses
(lit: horse five *ma-ri*)	

- For people: *myŏng, sa-ram, bun* (honorific)

hak-saeng yŏ-sŏt myŏng	six students
(lit: student six *myŏng*)	
a-hop sa-ram	nine people
(lit: nine *sa-ram*)	
kyo-su-nim han bun	one professor
(lit: professor one *bun*)	

- For papers: *jang*

jong-i da-sŏt jang	five sheets of paper
(lit: paper five *jang*)	

ki-ch'a-pyo du jang   two train tickets
(lit: train ticket two *yang*)

- For cups or glasses: *jan*
    maek-ju se jan   three glasses of beer
    (lit: beer three *jan*)
    k'ŏ-pi han jan   one cup of coffee
    (lit: coffee one *jan*)

- For books and notebooks: *kwŏn*
    ch'aek il-kop kwŏn   seven volumes of books
    (lit: book seven *kwŏn*)
    kong-ch'aek du kwŏn   two notebooks
    (lit: notebook two *kwŏn*)

- For bottles: *byŏng*
    maek-ju da-sŏt byŏng   five bottles of beer
    (lit: beer five *byŏng*)

- For cars: *dae*
    ch'a han dae   one car
    (lit: car one *dae*)

- For floors of a building: *ch'ŭng*
    10 ch'ŭng   10th floor
    (lit: 10 *ch'ŭng*)

- For flowers and grapes: *song-i*
    jang-mi-kkot han song-i   one rose
    (lit: rose flower one *song-i*)

- For pencils and rifles: *ja-ru*
    yŏn-pil du ja-ru   two pencils
    (lit: pencil two *ja-ru*)

Pronouns

First and second person pronouns are categorised depending upon the level of politeness between the conversing parties.

English pronouns are frequently represented in Korean as nouns. The noun, *sŏn-saeng-nim* (teacher), for example, is used to mean `you' or sometimes `he/she'. There are also various other nouns used to represent `this' or `that'.

The category of pronoun is identified by a suffix. Subject pronouns end with *-nŭn*, object pronouns end with *-rŭl*, and possessive pronouns end with *-ŭi*:

Singular			
1st Person	I	*jŏ-*	저–
		na- (inf)	나–
2nd Person	you	*dang-shin-*	당신–
		nŏ- (inf)	너–
3rd Person	he, she, it	*kŭ-bun-, kŭ-yŏ-ja-bun-,*	그분– 그여자분–
		kŭ-nŭn-, kŭ-nyŏ-,	그는 그녀–
		kŭ-gŏ- (inf)	그것–
Plural			
1st Person	we	*u-ri-* (form & inf)	우리–
2nd Person	you	*dang-shin-dŭl-*	당신들–
		nŏ-hŭi- (inf)	너희–
3rd Person	they	*kŭ-bun-dŭl-*	그분들–
		kŭ-dŭ- (inf)	그들–

Adjectives

Korean adjectives either precede a noun or another adjective as in English, or they follow the subject and behave like a verb in which case they are modified.

cold
This is cold water.
The water is cold.

ch'an
ch'an-mul-im-ni-da
mul-i ch'a-yo

big
This is a big car.
The car is big.

k'ŭn
i-gŏ-sŭn k'ŭn ch'a-im-ni-da
ch'a-ga k'ŭm-ni-da

Verbs

Korean verbs have no special forms to indicate person or number. A verb stem plus a suffix indicate the tense of the verb, the mood of the verb, the relationship between the speakers and whether the sentence is a question. These suffixes may have different forms depending upon whether they follow a vowel or consonant.

	Suffix	Phrase	
Verb stem	---	*mŏk-da*	eat
Honorific	*-shi-*	*jap-su-shin-da*	is eating
Present	*-nŭn-*	*mŏk-nŭn-da*	eat
Past	*-ŏd-*	*mŏk-ŏd-da*	ate
Future	*-ked-*	*mŏk-ked-da*	will eat
Humble	*-sŭm-ni-*	*mŏk-ged-sŭm-ni-da*	I will eat.
Interrogative	*-kka*	*dŭ-syŏd-sŭm-ni-kka*	Did you eat?

To Be & To Have

Korean does not use specific verbs for `to be' and `to have'.
Instead, it has two verbs which translate the English words `is',
`am', `are' and `be'. These distinguish between `is', *im-ni-da/i-
e-yo* (inf), meaning `to be/equals' and `is', *iss-sŭm-ni-da/iss-ŏ-yo*
(inf), meaning `exists/stays':

He is a dentist.	*ch'i-kwa ŭi-sa-im-ni-da*
	ch'i-kwa ŭi-sa-ye-yo (inf)
	(lit: dentist is)

The newspaper is	*shin-mun-i jŏ-ki-e iss-sŭm-ni-da*
over there.	*shin-mun-i jŏ-ki-e iss-ŏ-yo* (inf)
	(lit: newspaper over there exists)

`Has' or `got' is expressed as `exists':

I have a car.	*ch'a iss-sŭm-ni-da*
	ch'a iss-ŏ-yo (inf)
	(lit: car exists)

Particles

Korean subject and object nouns are not always apparent from
the word order. Particles are used to indicate the grammatical
relationship of each noun to the verb or other words in the
sentence. Particles also replace the role of English prepositions
such as `in', `to' or `at'.

A noun used as the subject is followed by the particle *-ka* when
the noun ends with a vowel, or *-i* when it ends with a consonant.
A noun used as a direct object is followed by the particle *-rŭl/-ŭl*.

The particle *-nŭn/-ŭn*, is used when one idea in the sentence is in contrast with another. In this case it replaces *-ka*, *-i*, *rŭl* and *ŭl*.

(although it is small) It is heavy.	*(jŏk-ji-man) kŭ-gŏ-sŭn mu-gŏp-da*
(although it is spring) The weather is cold.	*(bom-i-ji-man) nal-shi-nŭn ch'a-gŏp-da*

Adverbs

Korean adverbs are generally placed in front of the verb they modify:

brightly
The sun shone brightly.

bal-ge
haet-byŏt-i bal-ge bi-ch'u-i-da
(lit: sun brightly shone)

very
This wine is very good.

mae-u
sul-mat-i mae-u jo-sŭm-ni-da
(lit: wine very good is)

too much
I've eaten too much.

nŏ-mu manh-i
nŏ-mu manh-i mŏ-gŏss-sŭm-ni-da
(lit: too much eaten)

Questions & Statements

Like English, Korean uses tonal variation to distinguish between statements, exclamations, imperatives and questions. Use rising or falling intonation as you would in English:

| I am going to Korea. | *Han-guk-e ka-yo* |
| You're going to Korea! | *Han-guk-e ka-yo!* |

Tonal variation distinguishes between two different types of question:

- seeking details (falling intonation):
  | How many tickets do you want? | *p'yo myŏt jang dŭ-ril-kka-yo?* |

- seeking a `yes/no' reply (rising intonation):
  | Did you wait very long? | *o-rae ki-da-ri-syŏss-sŭm-ni-kka?* |
  | Are you going to Korea? | *Han-guk-e ka-yo?* |

Question Words

why	*wae*	왜
who	*nu-gu*	누구
which	*ŏ-nŭ*	어느
what	*mu-ŏt*	무엇
where	*ŏ-di*	어디
when	*ŏn-je*	언제
how	*ŏ-ttŏ-ke*	어떻게

Why has he gone?	*wae ka-syŏss-sŭm-ni-kka?*
Who did you meet?	*nu-gu-rŭl man-na-syŏss-sŭm-ni-kka?*
Which bus is it?	*ŏ-nu bŏ-sŭ im-ni-kka?*
What is this?	*mu-ŏt-im-ni-kka?*

Where does this bus go?	*i bŏ-sŭ ŏ-de-ro kam-ni-kka?*
When will we arrive?	*ŏn-je do-ch'ak-ham-ni-kka?*
How do I get there?	*kŏ-gi-e ŏ-ttŏ-ke kam-ni-kka?*

Negatives

'No' in Korean is *a-ni-o*. To make a sentence negative, the abbreviated version, *an*, is placed in front of the verb:

| I play. | *nol-a-yo* |
| I don't play. | *an nol-a-yo* |

GRAMMAR

an is not used in front of *iss-ŏ-yo*, the verb meaning `to exist'. Instead, there is a special verb, *ŏb-sŏ-yo*, which means `does not exist':

| I have a car. | *ch'a iss-sŭm-ni-da* |
| I don't have a car. | *ch'a ŏb-sŭm-ni-da* |

To express a strong negative, such as `never', `not at all' or `can't', use the word *mot*:

I can't go.	*mot kam-ni-da*
I never smoke.	*dam-bae-rŭl mot p'i-up-ni-da*
I don't eat any meat at all.	*ko-gi-rŭl jŏn-hyŏ mot mŏk-sŭm-ni-da*

Yes & No

Answering `yes/no' questions in Korea can lead to confusion and frustration. When Koreans agree with the speaker, they answer `yes' (*ye*). When they disagree, they answer `no' (*a-ni-o*). Depending upon the phrasing of the question, the answer could be opposite to that in English. To answer `yes' to a question, repeat the verb. To answer `no', repeat the verb using *an* as a prefix.

Do you like kimchi?	*kim-ch'i jo-a-ha-shim-ni-kka?*
Yes, I like kimchi.	*ye, kim-ch'i jo-a-ham-ni-da*
No, I don't like kimchi.	*a-ni-o, kim-ch'i an-jo-a-ham-ni-da*
Don't you like kimchi?	*kim-ch'i jo-a an-ha-shim-ni-kka?*
No, I don't like kimchi.	*ye, kim-ch'i an-jo-a-ham-ni-da* (lit: yes, I don't like kimchi)
Yes, I do like kimchi.	*a-ni-o, kim-ch'i jo-a-ham-ni-da* (lit: no, I do like kimchi)

Modals

A modal is a phrase that modifies the mood of a verb by expressing ability, necessity, desire or need. In Korean it is always added to the verb as a suffix.

can	**... su iss-ŏ-yo**
I can buy.	*sal su iss-sŭm-ni-da*
I can't buy.	*sal su ŏb-sŭm-ni-da*
Can I buy?	*sal su iss-sŭm-ni-kka?*

want	**... ko ship-sŭm-ni-da**
I want to go.	*ka-go ship-sŭm-ni-da*
I don't want to go.	*an ka-go ship-sŭm-ni-da*
Do you want to go?	*ka-go ship-sŭm-ni-da?*

must/have to

I must go.
I must not go.
Must I go?

... ya ham-ni-da

ka-ya ham-ni-da
ka-myŏn an doem-ni-da
ka-ya ham-ni-da?

would

She/he would like to eat.
She/he would not like to eat now.
Would she/he like to eat now?

ha-go ship-da

jap-su-shi-ryŏ-go ham-ni-da
ji-kŭm an jap-su-shi-ryŏ-go ham-ni-da
ji-kŭm dŭ-shi-get-sŭm-ni-kka?

should/ought to

I should leave now.
You should not leave now.
Should I leave now?

hae-ya had-da

ji-kŭm ttŏu-na-ya ham-ni-da
ji-kŭm ttŏ-na-sŏn an-doem-ni-da
ji-kŭm ttŏ-na-ya ham-ni-kka?

Comparatives

To make comparisons, Koreans use the following comparative forms for both adjectives and adverbs:

-er
than

dŏ
-bo-da

This building is taller.
This building is taller than that building.

i kŏn-mul-i dŏ nop-sŭm-ni-da
*i kŏn-mul-ŭn jŏ kŏn-mul-bo-da
dŏ nop-sŭm-ni-da*

GRAMMAR

Superlatives

Korean uses one of two different words, both of which equate to `most' or to `-est'. The choice to use *je-il* or *ka-jang* is based on personal preference:

| Which is the longest river? | *ŏ-nŭ kŏt-i je-il kin kang-im-ni-kka?* |
| What is the most delicious food? | *mu-ŏt-i ka-jang mat-it-nŭn ŭm-shik-im-ni-kka?* |

Conjunctions

As in English, Korean usually joins two main clauses with the conjunctions `and', *kŭ-ri-go* or `but', which has the following three forms, *kŭ-rŏ-na*, *kŭ-ri-ji-man* or *... ji-man*.

And

A shortened form of *kŭ-ri-go* is used by attaching the last syllable, *-go*, as a suffix to the verb at the end of the first clause:

| I ate dinner and I listened to some music. | *jŏ-nyŏk-ŭl mŏk-go ŭm-ak-ŭl dŭl-ŏt-sŭm-ni-da* |

When 'and' is used between two or more nouns, it takes its particle forms. *-wa* follows a noun ending with a vowel and *-gwa* follows a noun ending with a consonant:

| I've lost my passport and my keys. | *yŏ-gwŏn-gwa yŏl-soe-rŭl i-rŏ-bŏ-ryŏss-sŭm-ni-da* |

GRAMMAR

But

When 'but' begins a sentence you may use either *kŭ-rŏ-na* or *kŭ-ri-ji-man*:

But I don't want to go.

kŭ-rŏ-na ka-go ship-ji an-sŭm-ni-da

In the middle of a sentence ... *ji-man* is usually used as a suffix to the verb at the end of the first clause:

Korean is difficult but it is interesting.

Han-guk-ŏ-nŭn ŏ-ryŏb-ji-man jae-mi-iss-sŭm-ni-da

GRAMMAR

Making Your Own Sentences

I don't drink alcohol.
 sŭ-rŭl an ma-shim-ni-da

술을 안 마십니다

Do you drink beer?
 *maek-ju-rŭl
 ma-shim-ni-kka?*

맥주를 마십니까?

I am going now.
 ji-gŭm kam-ni-da

지금 갑니다

I am tired.
 p'i-gon-ham-ni-da

피곤합니다

Are you tired?
 p'i-gon-ha-shim-ni-kka?

피곤하십니까?

The train leaves at 6 pm.
 *o-hu 6shi-e ki-ch'a-ka
 ttŏ-nam-ni-da*

오후 6시에 기차가 떠납니다

The train doesn't leave at 6 pm.
  o-hu 6shi-e ki-ch'a-ga an ttŏ-nam-ni-da
오후 6시에 기차가 안 떠납니다

I want to go to the bank.
  ŭn-haeng-e ka-go ship-sŭm-ni-da
은행에 가고 싶습니다

I need to send a letter.
  p'yŏn-ji-rŭl bo-nae-ya ham-ni-da
편지를 보내야 합니다

This hotel is very noisy.
  ho-t'el-i nŏ-mu shi-kkŭ-rŏ-wŏ-yo
호텔이 너무 시끄러워요

Do buses run on this street?
  i kil-e bŏ-sŭ-ga da-nim-ni-kka?
이 길에 버스가 다닙니까?

Do you rent bicycles here?
  ja-jŏn-gŏ bil-lil su iss-sŭm-ni-kka?
자전거 빌릴 수 있습니까?

Some Useful Words

about (approximately)	*dae-ryak*	대략
above	*wi-e*	위에
after	*hu-e*	후에
at	*-e*	-에
because	*wae-nya-ha-myŏn*	왜냐하면
before	*jŏn-e*	전에
for	*wi-ha-yŏ*	위하여
from	*bu-t'ŏ*	부터
here	*yŏ-gi*	여기
if	*man-yak*	만약

in	*an-e*	안에
near	*ka-kka-i*	가까이
or	*ho-gŭn*	흑은
out	*ba-ge*	밖에
that/those	*jŏ-gŏt/jŏ-gŏt-dŭl*	저것/저것들
there	*kŏ-gi*	거기
this/these	*i-gŏt/i-gŏt-dŭl*	이것/이것들
to	*-e-ge*	-에게
under	*mit-e*	밑에
with	*-ha-go (kat-ji)*	-하고 (같이)

GRAMMAR

Greetings & Civilities

Greetings

Korean has two levels of greetings – formal/polite and informal/casual. To greet a person correctly in Korean, you must first consider your relationship with them and then choose the appropriate greeting. The following verb endings are frequently used:

> *-m-ni-da/-m-ni-kka?*   —ㅂ 니다/—ㅂ 니까?
> (formal/polite)
> *-i-e-o/-se-yo?*   —이에오/—세요?
> (informal/casual)

- Formal/polite – for addressing older or senior people:
  Hello. How do you do?
  an-nyŏng-ha-shim-ni -kka?   안녕하십니까?

- Informal/casual – for addressing friends or younger/junior people:
  Hello. How do you do?
  an-nyŏng-ha-se-yo?   안녕하세요?

Koreans usually follow their greeting with further comments such as:

Pleased to see you.
  ch'ŏ-ŭm boep-kess-sŭm-ni-da   처음 뵙겠습니다
I will see you again.
  tto boep-kess-sŭm-ni-da   또 뵙겠습니다

- When answering the telephone, say:
  Hello.   *yŏ-bo-se-yo*   여보세요

- When you enter shops or restaurants, employees will greet you with:
  Welcome. Please come in.
  ŏ-sŏ o-se-yo   어서 오세요

- The following is used between people who know each other well:
  I haven't seen you for ages.
  o-rae-kan-man-im-ni-da   오래간만입니다
  How have you been keeping?
  yo-jŭm ŏ-ttŏ-ke ji-nae-shim-ni-kka?   요즘 어떻게 지내십니까?
  What are you doing these days?
  yo-jŭm mwŏ ha-shim-ni-kka?   요즘 뭐 하십니까?
  Where are you going?
  ŏ-di ka-shim-ni-kka?   어디 가십니까?

Goodbyes

Koreans have different ways of saying goodbye depending upon whether the speakers are staying at or departing a place. When both speakers are departing (such as after meeting for lunch), they use the same goodbye.

- When someone is leaving you, say:
  Goodbye.
  an-nyŏng-hi ka-ship-shi-yo   안녕히 가십시오
  an-nyŏng-hi ka-se-yo (inf)   안녕히 가세요
  (lit: go safely/well)

GREETINGS

- When leaving someone say:
    Goodbye.
    an-nyŏng-hi kye-ship-shi-yo   안녕히 계십시오
    an-nyŏng-hi kye-se-yo (inf)   안녕히 계세요
    (lit: stay safely/well)

The following expressions are used when someone is going out for a period of time. This applies to people living together temporarily, such as a tour party at a hotel, as well as those living together permanently.

See you later.
    da-nyŏ o-gess-sŭm-ni-da   다녀 오겠습니다
    (lit: I will go and return)
See you later.
    jal da-nyŏ o-ship-shi-yo   잘 다녀 오십시오
    (lit: please return safely)
Goodbye.
    an-nyŏng-hi kye-ship-shi-yo   안녕히 계십시오

- When you leave a shop, office or restaurant, say:
    Goodbye. Thank you.
    su-go ha-ship-shi-o. kam-sa-   수고 하십시오. 감사합니다
    ham-ni-da

Civilities
Koreans say `thank you' as often as Westerners and always reply with `don't mention it'.

- Formal – to older or senior people:
  Thank you (very much).
  (dae-dan-hi) kam-sa-ham-   (대단히) 감사합니다
  ni-da

- Informal – to friends or younger/junior people:
  Thank you.
  ko-ma-wǒ-yo   고마워요
  Don't mention it.
  ch'ǒn-man-e-yo   천만에요

In a Korean Household
If you are invited to dinner, your host is likely to say, `have plenty to eat, even though we have not prepared such a good meal'. Korean people usually prepare delicious meals for their visitors. Visitors are expected to eat a lot and to show their enjoyment.

Enjoy your meal.
  man-i jap-su-ship-shi-yo   많이 잡수십시오
  (lit: have plenty to eat)
That was a wonderful meal.
  mat-id-ke jal mǒ-gǒss-sǔm-   맛있게 잘 먹었습니다
  ni-da
  (lit: I have eaten a delicious meal)
I have had an enjoyable time.
  jae-mi-id-ke jal ji-naess-sǔm-   재미있게 잘 지냈습니다
  ni-da

GREETINGS

Use the following greetings if you are staying in a Korean household:

Good morning.
    an-nyŏng-hi ju-mu-syŏss-sŭm-   안녕히 주무셨습니까?
    ni-kka?
    (lit: did you sleep well?)

Good night.
    an-nyŏng-hi ju-mu-ship-shi-yo   안녕히 주무십시오
    (lit: have a good sleep)

Requests

When asking a question, Koreans use an honorific at the beginning of the sentence. (see Forms of Address, page 35, to choose the appropriate one for each situation.)

Excuse me, where is the bank?
    shil-lye-ham-ni-da, ŭn-haeng-i   실례합니다, 은행이
    ŏ-di-e iss-sŭm-ni-kka?   어디에 있습니까?
    (lit: excuse me, bank where is it?)
Excuse me, where is the ... Hotel?
    shil-lye-ham-ni-da, ... ho-t'el-i   실례합니다, ... 호텔이
    ŏ-di-e iss-sŭm-ni-kka?   어디에 있습니까?
    (lit: excuse me, ... Hotel where is it?)

Please come in.
    dŭl-ŏ o-ship-shi-yo   들어 오십시오
Please sit down.
    an-jŭ-ship-shi-yo   앉으십시오

Apologies

I am sorry.
mi-an-ham-ni-da   미안합니다

I am sorry for being late.
nŭ-jŏ-sŏ mi-an-ham-ni-da   늦어서 미안합니다

It doesn't matter.
kwaen-ch'an-sŭm-ni-da   괜찮습니다

I apologise.
joe-song-ham-ni-da   죄송합니다

Don't worry.
kŏk-jŏng ma-ship-shi-yo   걱정 마십시오

Forms of Address

Korea's early Confucian influence means that Koreans have exceptional zeal for education and self-advancement and a respect for knowledge. Therefore, when addressing a Korean it is important to use the form of address that reflects your relationship to them and their position. Korean adults rarely use first names when they address friends or acquaintances. They use the surname with the appropriate title or honorific. Introduce yourself by your name but not your title.

There are many subtle variations to the forms of address. The following are the most commonly used:

• When addressing an older or senior person, use their surname plus an honorific:
  Mr/Mrs/Miss/Ms ...
    ... *sŏn-saeng-nim*   ... 선생님
    (lit: ... teacher)
  Dr (Ph D) ...
    ... *bak-sa-nim*   ... 박사님

GREETINGS

Professor ...
... *kyo-su-nim* ... 교수님
How do you do, Mr/Mrs ...?
... *sŏn-saeng-nim an-nyŏng-ha-shim-ni-kka?* ... 선생님 안녕하십니까?

- When addressing a younger or junior person, use their surname preceded by Mr, Mrs or Miss. For a married woman, use the husband's surname:

Mr ...	*mi-sŭ-t'ŏ* ...	미스터 ...
Mrs ...	*mi-si-jŭ* ...	미시즈....
Miss ...	*mi-sŭ* ...	미스 ...

- For a young, unmarried woman, use the surname plus an honorific:

Miss ...	... *yang*	... 양

However, a Korean woman does not adopt her husband's surname when she marries. If a woman is married or in a high position, use her maiden name plus an honorific:

Mrs/Miss ...	... *yŏ-sa-nim*	... 여사님

Koreans live in a society where family and group take precedence over the individual. This collectivism is reflected in the many forms of common or everyday address.

GREETINGS

The following forms of address are used when addressing strangers in public places:

middle-aged woman
a-ju-mŏ-ni 아주머니
(lit: aunt)
middle-aged man
a-jŏ-si 아저씨
(lit: uncle)
elderly woman over 60
hal-mŏ-ni 할머니
(lit: grandmother)
elderly man over 60
hal-a-bŏ-ji 할아버지
(lit: grandfather)

When addressing someone in a business setting, it is very important to recognise their seniority by correct use of their title.

How do you do, ...	*Kim ... an-nyŏng-*	김 ... 안녕하십니까?
Kim?	*ha-shim-ni-kka?*	
Director	*i-sa-jang-nim*	이사장님
President	*sa-jang-nim*	사장님
Executive Director	*jŏn-mu-nim*	전무님
Department Head	*bu-jang-nim*	부장님
Section Head	*kwa-jang-nim*	과장님

Names
By tradition, Korean names are made up of three Chinese characters that are pronounced using three Korean syllables. More recently, Korean words are being used for names. The surname

GREETINGS

comes first and the remaining two syllables form the given names, of which one often identifies the generation. There are about 300 family names in Korea. Among the most common names are 김 (Kim), 이 (Lee), and 박 (Park).

Koreans do not refer to others by their given names. Even among siblings the younger ones do not address their elders by given names. Given names are used only among very close friends.

Body Language

You can leave a good impression with Koreans by making the right gestures of respect. When being introduced to or greeted by a Korean, initiate a bow, not a handshake or a kiss. The bow is made by bending from the waist to an angle of about 30°. In general a handshake is initiated by the more senior person.

Pointing or gesturing with one finger at somebody is considered impolite. Beckoning is done with the palm down and fluttering fingers.

Gifts

Giving gifts is customary in Korea in certain circumstances. Generally, when someone invites you to their home, you should take a gift.

If you are planning to visit a Korean family, consider taking one of your country's special products as a gift, such as food or an authentic souvenir. Wrap the gift and present it with two hands.

Please wrap this as a present.
   sŏn-mul-yong-i-ni-kka jal 선물용이니까 잘 포장해 주십시오
   p'o-jang-hae ju-ship-shi yo

It is just a small gift for you.
   jo-kŭ-man sŏn-mul-im-ni-da

조그만 선물입니다

May I open it now, please?
   yŏl-ŏ bo-a-do doem-ni-kka?

열어 보아도 됩니까?

It is very beautiful.
   ch'am ye-ppŭp-ni-da

참 예쁩니다

Some Useful Phrases

See you tomorrow.
   nae-il boep-gess-sŭm-ni-da

내일 뵙겠습니다

Have a safe trip.
   yŏ-haeng jal ha-ship-shi-yo

여행 잘 하십시오

Please give my regards to your
family.
   *ka-jok-e-ke an-bu-rŭl jŏn-hae
ju-ship-shi-yo*

가족에게 안부를 전해
주십시오

Cheers! (when raising your glass)
   kŏn-bae!

건배!

GREETINGS

Small Talk

Most Korean people are very friendly to Westerners. Don't be afraid to approach people for assistance. It's generally quite easy for foreign visitors to communicate with Koreans in urban areas as many Koreans speak English. In rural areas people tend to be more open, but language communication can be quite difficult. Koreans are more likely to understand written English better than spoken English.

Traditionally, Korean relationships have been based on Confucianism which emphasises respect for elders and superiors. Although younger Koreans are very westernised, remember to use correct formal expressions when talking to older Koreans. Also, Koreans are very sensitive to appearance. Appropriate dress is very important and it is unacceptable to eat while walking in public places.

A very popular venue in Korea for business and personal meetings is the `tearoom', 다방 (*da-bang*), where nonalcoholic beverages are served.

Meeting People

What is your name?
i-rŭm-i mu-ŏt-im-ni-kka?　　　이름이 무엇입니까?

My name is ...
je i-rŭm-ŭn ... im-ni-da　　　제 이름은 ... 입니다

Pleased to meet you.
ban-gap-sŭm-ni-da　　　반갑습니다

This is my business card.
je myŏng-ham-im-ni-da　　　제 명함입니다

40

This is my friend.
je ch'in-gŭ-im-ni-da   제 친구입니다

I wish to meet Mr Kim.
Kim sŏn-saeng-nim-ŭl man-na-   김 선생님을 만나고 싶습니다
go ship-sŭm-ni-da

Nationalities

Where are you from?
ŏ-nŭ na-ra-e-sŏ o-syŏss-sŭm-   어느 나라에서 오셨습니까?
ni-kka?

I am from ...   ... *e-sŏ wass-sŭm-*   ...에서 왔습니다
                     ni-da

Africa	*A-p'ŭ-ri-k'a*	아프리카
Australia	*Ho-ju*	호주
Austria	*O-sŭ-t'ŭ-ri-a*	오스트리아
Cambodia	*K'am-bo-di-a*	캄보디아
Canada	*K'ae-na-da*	캐나다
China	*Jung-guk*	중국
Denmark	*Den-ma-k'ŭ*	덴마크
England	*Yŏng-guk*	영국
Europe	*Yu-rŏp*	유럽
France	*P'ŭ-rang-sŭ*	프랑스
Germany	*Do-gil*	독일
Hong Kong	*Hong-k'ong*	홍콩
India	*In-do*	인도
Indonesia	*In-do-ne-shi-a*	인도네시아
Ireland	*A-il-raen-dŭ*	아일랜드
Italy	*I-t'al-li-a*	이탈리아
Japan	*Il-bon*	일본
Malaysia	*Mal-le-shi-a*	말레이시아

SMALL TALK

New Zealand	*Nyu-jil-laen-dŭ*	뉴질랜드
the Philippines	*P'il-ri-p'in*	필리핀
Singapore	*Shing-ka-p'o-rŭ*	싱가포르
South Africa	*Nam-a-p'ŭ-ri-k'a*	남아프리카
Spain	*Sŭ-p'e-in*	스페인
Sweden	*Sŭ-we-den*	스웨덴
Switzerland	*Sŭ-wi-sŭ*	스위스
Thailand	*T'ae-kuk*	태국
the Netherlands	*Ne-dŏl-ran-dŭ*	네델란드
the USA	*Mi-guk*	미국
Vietnam	*Be-t'ŭ-nam*	베트남

Age

How old are you?
    *yŏn-se-ga ŏ-ttŏ-ke doe-   연세가 어떻게 되십니까?
    shim-ni-kka?*
I am ... years old.
    ... sal-im-ni-da   ... 살입니다

(see Numbers & Amounts, page 161, for your particular age.)

Occupations

What do you do (for a living)?
    ji-gŏb-i mu-ŏt-im-ni-kka?   직업이 무엇입니까?
What is your monthly salary?
    wŏl-gŭp-i ŏl-ma-im-ni-kka?   월급이 얼마입니까?
Do you like working here?
    yŏ-gi-sŏ il-ha-nŭn kŏt-ŭl jo-a- 여기서 일하는 것을
    ha-shim-ni-kka?   좋아하십니까?

Do you enjoy your work?
ha-shi-nŭn i-rŭl jo-a-ha-shim-ni-kka? 하시는 일을 좋아하십니까?

What are you studying?
mu-sŭn kong-bu-rŭl ha-shim-ni-kka? 무슨 공부를 하십니까?

I am a/an ...	*jŏ-nŭn ...im-ni-da*	저는 ... 입니다
accountant	*hwa-gye-sa*	회계사
actor	*bae-u*	배우
artist	*hwa-ga*	화가
banker	*ŭn-haeng-wŏn*	은행원
business person	*sa-ŏp-ga*	사업가
carpenter	*mok-su*	목수
chef	*yo-ri-sa*	요리사
chemist	*yak-sa*	약사
doctor	*ŭi-sa*	의사
dentist	*ch'i-gwa-ŭi*	치과의
engineer	*ki-sa*	기사
factory worker	*kŭn-ro-ja*	근로자
farmer	*nong-bu*	농부
journalist	*ki-ja*	기자
lawyer	*byŏn-ho-sa*	변호사
mechanic	*jŏng-bi-sa*	정비사
musician	*ŭm-ak-ga*	음악가
nurse	*kan-ho-sa*	간호사
office worker/clerk	*sa-mu-wŏn*	사무원
parliamentarian	*jŏng-ch'i-ga*	정치가
police officer	*kyŏng-ch'al-gwan*	경찰관
retired person	*jŏng-nyŏn-t'oe-jik-ja*	정년퇴직자
scientist	*kwa-hak-ja*	과학자

shop assistant	*jŏm-wŏn*	점원
student	*hak-saeng*	학생
teacher	*kyo-sa*	교사
travel agent	*kwan-gwang-ŏp-ja*	관광업자
waiter	*we-i-t'ŏ*	웨이터
writer	*jak-ga*	작가

Religion

The four main streams of religion in Korea are shamanism, Buddhism, Confucianism and Christianity.

What is your religion?
jong-gyo-ga mu-ŏt-im-ni-kka?
종교가 무엇입니까?

I am ...   *jŏ-nŭn ... im-ni-da*
              저는 ... 입니다

Buddhist	*Bul-gyo shin-ja*	불교 신자
Catholic	*Ch'ŏn-ju-gyo shin-ja*	천주교 신자
Christian	*Ki-dok-gyo shin-ja*	기독교 신자
Confucian	*Yu-hak-do*	유학도
Hindu	*Hin-du-gyo shin-ja*	힌두교 신자
Jewish	*Yu-t'e-gyo shin-ja*	유태교 신자
Muslim	*I-sŭl-lam-gyo-do*	이슬람교도
shamanist	*sya-man-gyo-do*	샤만교도
Taoist	*Do-gyo shin-ja*	도교 신자
not religious	*mu-shin-ron-ja*	무신론자

Family

Are you married?
kyŏl-hon ha-syŏss-sŭm-ni-kka?　　　결혼 하셨습니까?

I am ...	*... -im-ni-da*	...입니다
single	*mi-hon-ja*	미혼자
married	*ki-hon-ja*	기혼자

This is my ...	*je ... -im-ni-da*	제 ...입니다
wife	*bu-in*	부인
husband	*nam-p'yŏn*	남편

I have ...	*... iss-sŭm-ni-da*	... 있습니다
I don't have ...	*... -ŏb-sŭm-ni-da*	... 없습니다
Do you have ...?	*... iss-sŭm-ni-kka?*	... 있습니까?
any children	*a-i-dŭl*	아이들
a boyfriend	*nam-ja-ch'in-gu*	남자친구
a girlfriend	*yŏ-ja-ch'in-gu*	여자친구

How many ... do	*... -myŏt myŏng iss-*	...몇 명
you have?	*sŭm-ni-kka?*	있습니까?
children	*a-i-dŭl*	아이들
brothers	*nam-ja-hyŏng-je-dŭl*	남자형제들
sisters	*yŏ-ja-hyŏng-je-dŭl*	여자형제들

Family Members

Korean terms for kinship are very complicated. There are separate
titles for paternal and maternal relatives, as well as for brothers
and sisters. Some generic family terms are shown in the following
list:

younger brother/sister	*dong-saeng*	동생
elder brother		
(called by younger brother)	*hyŏng*	형
(called by younger sister)	*o-ppa*	오빠
daughter	*ttal*	딸
family	*ka-jok*	가족
father	*a-bŏ-ji*	아버지
fiancé (m)	*yak-hon-ja*	약혼자
fiancée (f)	*yak-hon-nyŏ*	약혼녀
grandfather	*hal-a-bŏ-ji*	할아버지
grandmother	*hal-mŏ-ni*	할머니
husband	*nam-p'yŏn*	남편
mother	*ŏ-mŏ-ni*	어머니
parents	*bu-mo*	부모
elder sister		
(called by younger brother)	*nu-na*	누나
(called by younger sister)	*ŏn-ni*	언니
son	*a-dŭl*	아들
wife	*a-nae*	아내

Expressing Feelings

In Korean, `I am' is not specified when expressing feelings. The adjective on its own is sufficient.

I am ...

angry	*hwa nass-ŏ-yo*	화 났어요
cold	*ch'u-wŏ-yo*	추워요
grateful	*ko-ma-wŏ-yo*	고마워요
happy	*haeng-bok-hae-yo*	행복해요
hot	*dŏ-wŏ-yo*	더워요
hungry	*bae ko-p'a-yo*	배 고파요
in a hurry	*kŭm-hae-yo*	급해요
right	*ma-ja-yo*	맞아요
sad	*sŭl-p'ŏ-yo*	슬퍼요
sleepy	*jol-ryŏ-yo*	졸려요
sorry (condolence)	*an dwaess-ŏ-yo*	안 됐어요
thirsty	*mok mal-la-yo*	목 말라요
tired	*p'i-gon-hae-yo*	피곤해요
well	*kŏn-gang-hae-yo*	건강해요
worried	*kŏk-jŏng-i-e-yo*	걱정이에요
wrong	*jal-mot-haess-sŭm-ni-da*	잘못했습니다

Language Difficulties

I don't speak ...
... -rŭl mot-ham-ni-da ... 를 못합니다
I speak a little ...
... -rŭl jo-kŭm ham-ni-da ... 를 조금 합니다
Do you speak English?
Yŏng-ŏ-rŭl ha-shim-ni-kka? 영어를 하십니까?
Do you understand?
al-gess-sŭm-ni-kka? 알겠습니까?
I understand.
al-gess-sŭm-ni-da 알겠습니다

SMALL TALK

I don't understand.
mo-rŭ-gess-sŭm-ni-da   모르겠습니다

What does this mean?
i-ge mu-sŭn ttŭt-im-ni-kka?   이게 무슨 뜻입니까?

What does ... mean?
... mu-sŭn ttŭt-im-ni-kka?   ... 무슨 뜻입니까?

Would you repeat that?
*da-shi mal-sŭm-hae ju-shi-   다시말씀해
gess-sŭm-ni-kka?*   주시겠습니까?

Speak slowly, please.
*ch'ŏn-ch'ŏn-hi mal-sŭm-hae   천천히 말씀해 주십시오
ju-ship-shi-yo*

Please show me (in this book).
*(i ch'ae-ge-sŏ) bo-yŏ ju-   (이 책에서) 보여 주십시오
ship-shi-yo*

How do you say ...?
... ŏ-ttŏ-ke mal-ham-ni-kka?   ... 어떻게 말합니까?

Languages

I speak ...	*... -rŭl ham-ni-da*	...를 합니다
Bahasa Indonesia	*In-do-ne-shi-a-ŏ*	인도네시아어
Chinese	*Jung-guk-ŏ*	중국어
Dutch	*Ne-dŏl-lan-dŭ-ŏ*	네덜란드어
English	*Yŏng-ŏ*	영어
French	*P'ŭ-rang-sŭ-ŏ*	프랑스어
German	*Do-gil-ŏ*	독일어
Italian	*I-t'ae-li-ŏ*	이태리어
Japanese	*Il-bon-ŏ*	일본어
Korean	*Han-guk-ŏ*	한국어
Portuguese	*P'o-rŭ-t'u-gal-ŏ*	포르투갈어
Russian	*Rŏ-shi-a-ŏ*	러시아어

Spanish	*Sŭ-p'e-in-ŏ*	스페인어
Vietnamese	*Be-t'ŭ-nam-ŏ*	베트남어

Interests

What do you do in your spare time?

 ch'wi-mi-ga mŏ-shim-ni-kka?   취미가 무엇입니까?

I like ...	*... jo-a-ham-ni-da*	... 좋아합니다
I don't like ...	*... an jo-a-ham-ni-da*	... 안 좋아합니다
Do you like ...?	*... jo-a-ha-shim-ni-kka?*	... 좋아하십니까?
My favourite hobby is ...	*je ch'wi-mi-nŭn ...-im-ni-da*	제 취미는 ... 입니다
baseball	*ya-gu*	야구
basketball	*nong-gu*	농구
bicycle riding	*sa-i-k'ŭl*	사이클
classical/chamber music	*ko-jŏn-ŭm-ak/shil-nae-ak*	고전음악/실내악
discos/dancing	*di-sŭ-k'o/daen-sŭ*	디스코/댄스
films	*yŏng-hwa*	영화
fishing	*nak-shi*	낚시
shopping	*syo-p'ing*	쇼핑
golf	*kol-p'ŭ*	골프
hockey	*ha-k'i*	하키
horse riding	*sŭng-ma*	승마
karaoke	*no-rae-bang*	노래방
mountain climbing	*dŭng-san*	등산
music/popular music	*ŭm-ak/dae-jung-ŭm-ak*	음악/대중음악

SMALL TALK

playing sport	*un-dong*	운동
reading	*dok-sŏ*	독서
skiing	*sŭ-k'i*	스키
soccer	*ch'uk-gu*	축구
swimming	*su-yŏng*	수영
table tennis	*t'ak-gu*	탁구
tennis	*t'e-ni-sŭ*	테니스
travelling	*yŏ-haeng*	여행
volleyball	*bae-gu*	배구

Some Useful Words & Phrases

Yes.	*ne/ye*	네/예
No.	*a-ni-o/a-ni-yo*	아니오/아니요
Okay.	*jo-sŭm-ni-da*	좋습니다
Sure.	*hwak-shil-hae-yo*	확실해요
Of course.	*mul-lon-im-ni-da*	물론입니다
Maybe.	*a-ma*	아마
Really?	*jŏng-mal-im-ni-kka?*	정말입니까?

Lovely day!
  nal-shi-ga jo-sŭm-ni-da! 날씨가 좋습니다!
Beautiful, isn't it!
  ch'am a-rŭm-da-wŏ-yo! 참 아름다워요!
Interesting, isn't it!
  ch'am jae-mi-iss-ŏ-yo! 참 재미있어요!
Delicious, isn't it!
  ch'am mat-iss-ŏ-yo! 참 맛있어요!
What is this called?
  mu-ŏt-i-ra-go bu-rŭm-ni-kka? 무엇이라고 부릅니까?
No problem.
  mun-je ŏb-sŭm-ni-da 문제 없습니다

SMALL TALK

Never mind, it doesn't matter.
kŏk-jŏng ma-ship-shi-yo,
kwaen-ch'an-sŭm-ni-da

걱정 마십시오, 괜찮습니다

I know.
al-gess-sŭm-ni-da

알겠습니다

I don't know.
mo-rŭ-gess-sŭm-ni-da

모르겠습니다

Are you on holiday?
hyu-ga-im-ni-kka?

휴가입니까?

Do you live here?
yŏ-gi-e sa-shim-ni-kka?

여기에 사십니까?

Do you like it here?
yŏ-gi-rŭl jo-a-ha-shim-ni-kka?

여기를 좋아하십니까?

Are you ready?
jun-bi doe-ŏt-sŭm-ni-kka?

준비 되었습니까?

Let's go!
kap-shi-da!

갑시다

Please wait for me here.
yŏ-go-sŏ ki-da-ri-ship-shi-yo!

여기서 기다리십시오!

Don't smoke!
dam-bae p'i-u-ji ma-ship-
shi-yo!

담배 피우지 마십시오!

SMALL TALK

Getting Around

Korea is a small country with a high population density. It has one of the fastest growing economies and, therefore, it has developed an extensive, efficient and cost-effective public transport system. All of the tourist information centres and subway stations are signposted in English. The Korea National Tourism Corporation publishes tour guides and all transport timetables in English. These are available from the information centre at the airport. Despite the peak-hour crowds, travelling by public transport is the preferred method of seeing Korea.

Finding Your Way

Where is the ...?	... ŏ-di-e iss-sŭm-ni-kka?	... 어디에 있습니까?
I want to go to the ...	... -e ka-ryŏ-go ham-ni-da	...에 가려고 합니다
airport	kong-hang	공항
bus stop	bŏ-sŭ jŏng-ryu-jang	버스 정류장
express bus terminal	ko-sok-bŏ-sŭ t'ŏ-mi-nŏl	고속버스 터미널
ferry terminal	hwe-ri-ho t'ŏ-mi-nŏl	훼리호 터미널
subway station	ji-ha-ch'ŏl	지하철
taxi stand	t'aek-shi t'a-nŭn-got	택시 타는곳
ticket office	mae-p'yo-so	매표소

| tourist information centre | *kwan-gwang an-nae-so* | 관광 안내소 |
| train station | *ki-ch'a-yŏk* | 기차역 |

What time does the ... (leave)/(arrive)?	*... ŏn-je (ttŏ-nam-ni-kka)/(do-ch'ak-ham-ni-kka)?*	... 언제 (떠납니까)/ (도착합니까)?
bus	*bŏ-sŭ*	버스
express bus	*ko-sok-bŏ-sŭ*	고속버스
ferry	*hwe-ri-ho*	훼리호
plane	*bi-haeng-gi*	비행기
subway train	*ji-ha-ch'ŏl*	지하철
train	*ki-ch'a*	기차

Directions

When asking for directions, remember that Koreans give directions in relation to landmarks such as bridges, apartments, universities, hospitals, churches, department stores and hotels. They rarely use actual addresses or distances.

Where is ...?
   ... ŏ-di-e iss-sŭm-ni-kka?   ... 어디에 있습니까?
How do I get to ...?
   ... ŏ-ttŏ-ke kam-ni-kka?   ... 어떻게 갑니까?
Could you tell me where ... is?
   ... ŏ-di-e id-nŭn-ji al-lyŏ   ... 어디에 있는지 알려
   ju-shi-gess-sŭm-ni-kka?   주시겠습니까?
Is it far?
   mŏl-li iss-sŭm-ni-kka?   멀리 있습니까?
Is it near here?
   ka-kka-i iss-sŭm-ni-kka?   가까이 있습니까?

Can I walk there?
kŏ-rŏ kal su iss-sŭm-ni-ka?   걸어 갈 수 있습니까?

Can you show me (on this map)?
(i ji-do-e-sŏ) bo-yŏ ju-shi-gess-   (이 지도에서) 보여
sŭm-ni-kka?   주시겠습니까?

Are there other means of getting there?
kŏ-gi-e ka-nŭn da-rŭn kyo-   거기에 가는 다른
t'ong-p'yŏn-i iss-sŭm-ni-kka?   교통편이 있습니까?

Go straight ahead.
ttok-ba-ro ka-ship-shi-yo   똑바로 가십시오

Turn left ...	... *oen-jjok-ŭ-ro ka-ship-shi-yo*	... 왼쪽으로 가십시오
Turn right ...	... *o-rŭn-jjok-ŭ-ro ka-ship-shi-yo*	... 오른쪽으로 가십시오
at the next corner	*da-ŭm mo-t'ung-i-e-sŏ*	다음 모퉁이에서
at the traffic lights	*shin-ho-dŭng-e-sŏ*	신호등에서

Some Useful Words

above	*wi-e*	위에
around here	*i ju-byŏn-e*	이 주변에
behind	*dwi-e*	뒤에
below	*a-rae-e*	아래에
far	*mŏl-li*	멀리
in front of	*ap-e*	앞에
near	*ka-kka-i*	가까이
opposite	*ban-dae*	반대
to the side	*yŏp-ŭ-ro*	옆으로
east	*dong-jjok*	동쪽
west	*sŏ-jjok*	서쪽

| north | *buk-jjok* | 북쪽 |
| south | *nam-jjok* | 남쪽 |

Buying Tickets

You must book at least two weeks ahead if you want to travel during national holidays. (see Time, Dates & Festivals, page 153, for a list of national holidays and festivals.)

I would like a/an ... ticket.	... *-p'yo han-jang ju-ship-shi-yo*	... 표 한장 주십시오
How much is a/an ...?	... *-p'yo han-jang ŏl-ma-im-ni-kka?*	... 표 한장 얼마입니까?
one-way	*p'yŏn-do*	편도
return	*wang-bok*	왕복
entrance	*ip-jang*	입장
reserved seat	*jwa-sŏk*	좌석
unreserved seat	*ip-sŏk*	입석

I want to go to ...
 ... *ka-ryŏ-go ham-ni-da*　　　...가려고 합니다
How much is it to go to ...?
 ... *-ka-nŭn-de ŏl-ma-im-ni-kka?*　　...가는데 얼마입니까?
I would like to book a seat to ...
 ... *jwa-sŏ-gŭl ye-yak-hae ju-ship-shi-yo*　　... 좌석을 예약해
　　　　　　　　　주십시오
Where can I buy a ticket for ...?
 ... *-p'yo-rŭl ŏ-di-sŏ sal su iss-sŭm-ni-kka?*　　...표를 어디서 살 수
　　　　　　　　　있습니까?
Where is the ticket window for ...?
 ... *mae-p'yo-gu-ga ŏ-di-e iss-sŭm-ni-kka?*　　... 매표구가 어디에
　　　　　　　　　있습니까?

Chonju	*Jŏn-ju*	전주
Inch'ŏn	*In-ch'ŏn*	인천
Kwangju	*Kwang-ju*	광주
Kyŏngju	*Kyŏng-ju*	경주
Pusan	*Bu-san*	부산
Seoul	*Sŏ-ul*	서울
Taegu	*Dae-gu*	대구
Taejon	*Dae-jŏn*	대전

Can I reserve a seat?
jwa-sŏ-gŭl ye-yak-hae ju-shi-gess-sŭm-ni-kka?

좌석을 예약해 주시겠습니까?

Please refund my ticket.
je p'yo-rŭl ban-hwan-hae ju-ship-shi-yo

제 표를 반환해 주십시오

Is there a discount for ...?
... hal-in-p'yo iss-sŭm-ni-kka?

... 할인표 있습니까?

a child	*ŏ-rin-i*	어린이
a student	*hak-saeng*	학생
an elderly person	*no-in*	노인

Air

Korean Air and Asiana Airlines serve the domestic flight network linking 14 major cities in Korea. Bookings and timetables are available from the airline offices and the travel agencies. The airfares are reasonably priced as most flights take less than one hour within Korea. Allow enough time to get to the airport, especially in peak-hour traffic.

Is there a flight to ...?
... -e ka-nŭn hang-gong-p'yŏn iss-sŭm-ni-kka?

... 에 가는 항공편 있습니까?

When is the next flight to ...?
... -e ka-nŭn da-ŭm hang-gong-p'yŏn-i ŏn-je iss-sŭm-ni-kka?

...에 가는 다음 항공편이 언제 있습니까?

What day does the flight to ... leave?
... -e ka-nŭn hang-gong-p'yŏn-i myŏ-ch'il-nal iss-sŭm-ni-kka?

... 에 가는 항공편이 며칠날 있습니까?

What is the airfare to ...?
... -kka-ji hang-gong-yo-gŭm-i ŏl-ma-im-ni-kka?

...까지 항공요금이 얼마입니까?

Cheju Island	*Je-ju-do*	제주도
Kwangju	*Kwang-ju*	광주
Mokp'o	*Mok-p'o*	목포
P' ohang	*P'o-hang*	포항
Pusan	*Bu-san*	부산
Seoul	*Sŏ-ul*	서울
Taegu	*Dae-gu*	대구
Ulsan	*Ul-san*	울산

How long does the flight take?
bi-haeng shi-gan-i ŏl-ma-na kŏl-lim-ni-kka?

비행 시간이 얼마나 걸립니까?

GETTING AROUND

How much luggage may I take?
jim-ŭl ŏl-ma-na ka-ji-go kal su iss-sŭm-ni-kka?

짐을 얼마나 가지고 갈 수 있습니까?

What time must I check in?
myŏt shi-e ch'e-k'ŭ-hae-ya ham-ni-kka?

몇 시에 체크해야 합니까

Do I have to confirm my reservation?
ye-ya-gŭl da-shi hwa-gin-hae-ya ham-ni-kka?

예약을 다시 확인해야 합니까?

May I have a window seat?
ch'ang-yŏp jwa-sŏ-gŭ-ro ju-shi-gess-sŭm-ni-kka?

창옆 좌석으로 주시겠습니까?

I want a non-smoking seat, please.
kŭm-yŏn-sŏ-gŭl ju-ship-shi-yo

금연석을 주십시오

What is the ... time?	... *myŏt shi-e ham-ni-kka?*	... 몇 시에 합니까?
What is the ... gate?	... *-ke-i-t'ŭ-ga ŏ-di-e iss-sŭm-ni-kka?*	... 게이트가 어디에 있습니까?
departure	*ch'ul-bal*	출발
arrival	*do-ch'ak*	도착

Some Useful Words

airport tax	*kong-hang-se*	공항세
boarding pass	*t'ap-sŭng-gwŏn*	탑승권
customs	*se-gwan*	세관
aeroplane	*hang-gong-gi*	항공기

Subway

The subway is the most convenient and efficient mode of transport in both Seoul and Pusan. Station names are clearly marked in English and in-train announcements are made in both English and Korean. Tickets are sold in stations at ticket windows and through vending machines.

Where is the ... subway station?	... -ji-ha-ch'ŏl yŏ-gi ŏ-di-e iss-sŭm-ni-kka?	...지하철 역이 어디에 있습니까?
Line One	*il ho-sŏn*	1호선
Line Two	*i ho-sŏn*	2호선
Line Three	*sam ho-sŏn*	3호선
Line Four	*sa ho-sŏn*	4호선
Line Five	*o ho-sŏn*	5호선

Where do I change for Line ...?
   ... -ho-sŏn-ŭl ŏ-di-sŏ ka-ra
   t'am-ni-kka?

...호선을 어디서
갈아 탑니까?

Which line do I take to go to ...?
   ... ka-ryŏ-myŏn myŏt ho-sŏn
   t'a-ya ham-ni-kka?

... 가려면 몇 호선
타야 합니까?

Does this train go to the Seoul
Express Bus Terminal?
   i ki-ch'a-ga Sŏ-ul ko-sok-bŏ-sŭ
   t'ŏ-mi-nŏl-e kam-ni-kka?

이 기차가 서울
고속버스 터미널에
갑니까?

At which station do I get off for ...?
   ...-ka-ryŏ-myŏn ŏ-nŭ yŏ-ge-sŏ
   nae-ryŏ-ya ham-ni-kka?

... 가려면 어느
역에서 내려야
합니까?

May I have a subway map in
English, please?
> *yŏng-mun ji-ha-ch'ŏl no-sŏn-*
> *do-ga iss-sŭm-ni-kka?*

영문 지하철 노선도가
있습니까?

Where is the nearest subway
station?
> *kŭn-ch'ŏ ji-ha-ch'ŏl yŏ-gi ŏ-di-*
> *e iss-sŭm-ni-kka?*

근처 지하철 역이
어디에 있습니까?

Bus

Korea has extensive bus services, ranging from inexpensive local
buses to more expensive deluxe buses. Bus routes are colour-
coded and numbered, but they don't show destinations in English.

Where can I catch a ... bus?	... *bŏ-sŭ ŏ-di-sŏ* *t'am-ni-kka?*	... 버스 어디서 탑니까?
local city	*il-ban*	일반
city express	*jwa-sŏk*	좌석
deluxe city express	*t'ŭk-byŏl jwa-sŏk*	특별 좌석
inter-city	*shi-oe*	시외
long distance express	*ko-sok*	고속
long distance deluxe express	*u-dŭng ko-sok*	우등 고속

Do the buses pass frequently?
bŏ-sŭ-ga ja-ju iss-sŭm-ni-kka?　　버스가 자주 있습니까?

Where can I buy bus tokens?
t'o-k'ŭn ŏ-di-sŏ sam-ni-kka?　　토큰 어디서 삽니까?

Do you sell bus tokens?
t'o-k'ŭn p'a-shim-ni-kka?　　토큰 파십니까?

How much is the fare?
ŏl-ma-im-ni-kka?　　얼마입니까?

I've missed the bus.
bŏ-sŭ-rŭl no-ch'yŏss-sŭm-ni-da　　버스를 놓쳤습니다

What time is the ... bus?	... bŏ-sŭ myŏt shi-e iss-sŭm-ni-kka?	... 버스 몇 시에 있습니까?
next	da-ŭm	다음
first	ch'ŏt	첫
last	ma-ji-mak	마지막

Does this bus go to ...?
i bŏ-sŭ ...-e kam-ni-kka?　　이 버스 ... 에 갑니까?

I want to get off at ...
...-e-sŏ nae-ryŏ ju-ship-shi-yo　　... 에서 내려 주십시오

Could you let me know when we get to ...?
...-e ka-ryŏ-myŏn ŏ-di-sŏ nae-ri-nŭn-ji al-lyŏ ju-shi-gess-sŭm-ni-kka?　　... 에 가려면 어디서 내리는지 알려 주시겠습니까?

Where can I get a bus to ...?
...-e ka-nŭn bŏ-sŭ-rŭl ŏ-di-sŏ t'am-ni-kka?　　... 에 가는 버스를 어디서 탑니까?

Do I need to change buses to go to ...?
...-e ka-ryŏ-myŏn bŏ-sŭ-rŭl kal-a-t'a-ya ham-ni-kka?　　... 에 가려면 버스를 갈아타야 합니까?

Ch'angdŏk Palace	*Ch'ang-dŏk-gung*	창덕궁
City Hall	*shi-chŏng*	시청
East Gate	*Dong-dae-mun*	동대문
Itaewon	*I-t'ae-wŏn*	이태원
South Gate	*Nam-dae-mun*	남대문
Seoul Train Station	*Sŏ-ul-yŏk*	서울역

Train

There is an extensive network of passenger trains across Korea.
These are reasonably fast, reliable and are moderately priced.
There are four classes of trains, from `local trains', 비둘기호
(*bi-dul-gi-ho*), which stop at all stations (you cannot book seats)
through to super-express trains which must be booked up to two
weeks in advance during weekends and national holidays.

Is it an express train?
   tŭk-gŭp yŏl-ch'a-im-ni-kka?   특급 열차입니까?
What is this station called?
   yŏk i-rŭm-i mu-ŏt-im-ni-kka?   역 이름이 무엇입니까?
What is the next station?
   da-ŭm yŏk i-rŭm-ŭn mu-ŏt-im-   다음 역 이름은
   ni-kka?   무엇입니까?
Does this train stop at ...?
   ...yŏk-e-sŏ mŏm-ch'um-ni-kka?   ...역에서 멈춥니까?
Which platform do I go to?
   ŏ-nŭ p'ŭl-raet-p'om-e-sŏ t'a-   어느 플랫폼에서 타야
   ya doem-ni-kka?   됩니까?

Some Useful Words

| train | *ki-ch'a* | 기차 |
| train station | *ki-ch'a-yŏk* | 기차역 |

dining car	*shik-dang-ch'a*	식당차
local train (stops all stations)	*bi-dul-gi-ho (wan-haeng)*	비둘기호 (완행)
limited express train	*t'ong-il-ho*	통일호
express train	*mu-gung-hwa-ho*	무궁화호
super-express train	*sae-ma-ul-ho*	새마을호

Taxi

Taxis are plentiful and reasonably priced. However, due to high demand in the cities, it can be very difficult to find a vacant one. There are two sizes of standard taxis – small and medium. It may be necessary to agree on a flat fare before setting off, especially during peak hour.

There are also deluxe taxis, 모범 (*mo-bŏm*), which are black with a yellow sign on the roof. These are more readily available but charge about three times the standard taxi fare.

For inter-city or long-distance trips, you should negotiate the fare before you depart.

Where can I get a taxi?
ŏ-di-sŏ t'aek-shi-rŭl t'am-ni-kka?   어디서 택시를 탑니까?

Can you take me to ...?	*... ka ju-ship-shi-yo?*	... 가 주십시오?
Kimpo Airport	*Kim-p'o bi-haeng-jang*	김포 비행장
Seoul Express Bus Terminal	*Sŏ-ul ko-sok-bŏ-sŭ t'ŏ-mi-nŏl*	서울 고속버스 터미널
Seoul Station	*Sŏ-ul-yŏk*	서울역

How long does it take to get there?
kŏ-gi-kka-ji ŏl-ma-na kŏl-lim-ni-kka? 거기까지 얼마나 걸립니까?

How much does it cost to go to ...?
... -kka-ji ŏl-ma-im-ni-kka? ... 까지 얼마입니까?

It's too much.
nŏ-mu bi-sam-ni-da 너무 비쌉니다

Instructions

Here is fine, thank you.
jo-sŭm-ni-da, kam-sa-ham-ni-da 좋습니다. 감사합니다

Continue.
kye-sok ka-ship-shi-yo 계속 가십시오

Stop here.
yŏ-gi se-wŏ ju-ship-shi-yo 여기 세워 주십시오

Over there.
jŏ-gi-e 저기에

Please slow down.
ch'ŏn-ch'ŏn-hi ka-ship-shi-yo 천천히 가십시오

Please hurry.
ppal-li ka ju-ship-shi-yo 빨리 가 주십시오

Please wait here.
yŏ-gi-sŏ ki-da-ryŏ ju-ship-shi-yo 여기서 기다려 주십시오

Car

With Korea's dense population, high accident rate and car ownership, it is not advisable to drive yourself. If you want to rent a car, consider hiring a driver. For those who must drive themselves, the following will help:

Where can I rent a car?
ren-t'ŏ-k'a hoe-sa-ga ŏ-di iss-sŭm-ni-kka? | 렌터카 회사가 어디 있습니까?

I'd like to rent ... | *... -rŭl bil-li-go ship-sŭm-ni-da* | ...를 빌리고 싶습니다

a small car	*so-hyŏng-ch'a*	소형차
a middle-sized car	*jung-hyŏng-ch'a*	중형차
a large car	*dae-hyŏng-ch'a*	대형차
an automatic car	*ja-dong-gi-ŏ-ch'a*	자동기어차
a manual car	*su-dong-gi-ŏ-ch'a*	수동기어차

What is the ... rate? | *... ren-t'ŭ-ryo-ga ŏl-ma-im-ni-kka?* | ... 렌트료가 얼마입니까?

daily	*ha-ru*	하루
weekly	*il-ju-il*	일주일
monthly	*han-dal*	한달

Does that include insurance?
bo-hŏm-ryo-do p'o-ham doe-ŏt-sŭm-ni-kka? | 보험료도 포함 되었습니까?

Can you arrange a driver?
un-jŏn-gi-sa-rŭl ju-sŏn-hae ju-shi-gess-sŭm-ni-kka? | 운전기사를 주선해 주시겠습니까?

Can I have a road map?
do-ro ji-do-rŭl ju-shi-gess-sŭm-ni-kka? | 도로 지도를 주시겠습니까?

Where's the nearest petrol station?
i kŭn-ch'ŏ ju-yu-so-ga ŏ-di-e iss-sŭm-ni-kka? | 이 근처 주유소가 어디에 있습니까?

Traffic Signs

Korea has many pictorial traffic signs which are similar to standard international signs. However, some traffic signs and notices also include words.

버스 정류장	**BUS STOP**
주의	**CAUTION**
위험!	**DANGER!**
입구	**ENTRANCE**
출구	**EXIT**
양보	**GIVE WAY**
진입금지	**NO ENTRY**
주차금지	**NO PARKING**
일방통행	**ONE WAY**
통행금지	**ROAD CLOSED**
천천히	**SLOW DOWN**
멈춤	**STOP**

Domestic Ferry/Hydrofoil

Boat travel is most extensive along the the south and south-west coasts, including the Hallyo Waterway National Park, and from the mainland to the many small islands off the coast.

Where is the ...?	... *ŏ-di-e iss-sŭm-ni-kka?*	... 어디에 있습니까?
ferry terminal	*hwe-ri t'ŏ-mi-nŏl*	훼리 터미널
pier	*bu-du*	부두
ticket office	*mae-p'yo-so*	매표소

When does the next ferry leave for ...?
... -ka-nŭn da-ŭm hwe-ri-ga ŏn-
je iss-sŭm-ni-kka?
... 가는 다음 훼리가
언제 있습니까?

What time do we arrive at ...?
... myŏt shi-e do-ch'ak-ham-
ni-kka?
... 몇 시에 도착합니까?

Cheju	*Je-ju-do*	제주도
Mokp'o	*Mok-p'o*	목포
Pusan	*Bu-san*	부산
Sogwipo	*Sŏ-kwi-p'o*	서귀포
Yosu	*Yŏ-su*	여수

Paperwork

address	*ju-so*	주소
age	*yŏn-ryŏng*	연령
birth certificate	*ch'ul-saeng jŭng-*	
	myŏng-sŏ	출생 증명서
border	*kuk-gyŏng*	국경
customs	*se-gwan*	세관

GETTING AROUND

date of birth	*saeng-nyŏn-wŏl-il*	생년월일
driving licence	*un-jŏn-myŏn-hŏ-jŭng*	운전면허증
identification	*shin-bun-jŭng*	신분증
immigration	*i-min*	이민
itinerary	*yŏ-haeng-il-jŏng*	여행일정
marital status	*kyŏl-hon-yŏ-bu*	결혼여부
name	*sŏng-myŏng*	성명
nationality	*kuk-jŏk*	국적
occupation	*jik-ŏp*	직업
passport	*yŏ-gwŏn*	여권
passport number	*yŏ-gwŏn bŏn-ho*	여권 번호
place of birth	*ch'ul-saeng-ji*	출생지
(port of) arrival/departure	*ip-guk/ch'ul-guk (jang-so)*	입국/출국(장소)
reason for travel	*yŏ-haeng-mok-jŏk*	여행목적
registration	*dŭng-rok*	등록
religion	*jong-gyo*	종교
sex (gender)	*sŏng-byŏl*	성별
tour	*kwan-gwang*	관광
... visa	*... bi-ja*	... 비자
business	*sa-ŏp*	사업
extension	*yŏn-jang*	연장
journalist	*ki-ja*	기자
tourist	*yŏ-haeng-ja*	여행자
visitor's	*bang-mun-ja*	방문자
student	*hak-saeng*	학생
temporary resident	*im-shi-gŏ-ju-ja*	임시거주자
working	*ch'wi-ŏp*	취업

Signs

위험	**DANGER**
입구	**ENTRANCE**
출구	**EXIT**
촬영금지	**NO PHOTOGRAPHS**
금연	**NO SMOKING**
출입금지	**NO ENTRY**
횡단 보도	**PEDESTRIANS CROSSING**
보행자 전용 도로	**PEDESTRIANS ONLY**
횡단 금지	**PEDESTRIANS PROHIBITED**
정지	**STOP**

Some Useful Words & Phrases

The (train) is ...	*...-(ki-ch'a)ga*	. . . (기차)가
delayed	*yŏn-ch'ak doe-ŏss-sŭm-ni-da*	연착 되었습니다
cancelled	*ch'wi-so doe-ŏss-sŭm-ni-da*	취소 되었습니다
on time	*je shi-gan-e do-ch'ak-ham-ni-da*	제 시간에 도착합니다

How long will it be delayed?
ŏl-ma-dong-an yŏn-ch'ak-doem-ni-kka?   얼마동안 연착됩니까?

Do I need to change?
kal-a t'a-ya doem-ni-kka?   갈아 타야 됩니까?

You must change trains/buses.
*ki-ch'a/bŏ-sŭ-rŭl kal-a t'a-ya
doem-ni-da*

기차/버스를 갈아
타야 됩니다

How long does the trip take?
ŏl-ma-na kŏl-lim-ni-kka?

얼마나 걸립니까?

Is it a direct route?
kot-jang kam-ni-kka?

곧장 갑니까?

Is that seat taken?
ja-ri iss-sŭm-ni-kka?

자리 있습니까?

Where is the toilet?
*hwa-jang-shil-i ŏ-di-e iss-sŭm-
ni-kka?*

화장실이 어디에
있습니까?

Where is the waiting-room?
*dae-gi-so-ga ŏ-di-e iss-sŭm-ni-
kka?*

대기소가 어디에
있습니까?

cancel	*ch'wi-so-ha-da*	취소하다
deposit	*ye-ch'i-gŭm*	예치금
fastest route	*ppa-rŭn gil*	빠른 길
first class	*il-dŭng-sŏk*	일등석
lost property	*bun-shil-mul bo-gwan-sŏ*	분실물 보관소
non-smoking	*kŭm-yŏn-sŏk*	금연석
seat	*jwa-sŏk*	좌석
short route	*ji-rŭm gil*	지름 길
smoking	*hŭp-yŏn*	흡연
ticket	*p'yo*	표
timetable	*shi-gan-p'yo*	시간표
travel agency	*yŏ-haeng-sa*	여행사

Accommodation

There are five major types of accommodation in Korea – hotels, *yŏgwan* (Korean-style inns), *yŏinsuk* (small Korean-style inns), *minbak* (rooms in private houses) and youth hostels. Hotels range from international five-star standard to basic accommodation. They are classified by the `Rose of Sharon' (the national flower of Korea) instead of stars. The top quality hotels have five roses.

Rose of Sharon

Yŏgwans are a good way to experience the Korean way of life. You can find them everywhere in Korea and they are generally much cheaper than hotels. However, most owners only speak Korean, and remember to remove your shoes at the door!

For those travelling on a minimum budget, youth hostels and minbak are worth considering. During the summer, Korea has some limited camping areas and facilities. In Seoul, youth hostels are slowly disappearing, and can be more expensive than yŏgwans and business-class hotels.

As Koreans now enjoy a higher standard of living, they travel much more during holiday periods. Book your accommodation ahead if you are travelling during July (especially at beach resorts) or during public holidays.

Finding Accommodation

Where is a ...?	... ŏ-di-e iss-sŭm-ni-kka?	... 어디에 있습니까?
camp site	k'aem-p'ŭ-jang	캠프장
hotel	ho-t'el	호텔
minbak	min-bak	민박
yŏgwan	yŏ-gwan	여관
yŏinsuk	yŏ-in-suk	여인숙
youth hostel	yu-sŭ ho-sŭ-t'el	유스 호스텔

Can you recommend a ...?	... ch'u-ch'ŏn-hae ju-shi-gess-sŭm-ni-kka?	... 추천해 주시겠습니까?
I'm looking for a...	... wŏn-ham-ni-da	... 원합니다
cheap hotel	san ho-t'el	싼 호텔
clean hotel	kkae-kkŭt-han ho-t'el	깨끗한 호텔
good hotel	ko-gŭp hot'el	고급 호텔
hotel near here	i kŭn-ch'ŏ ho-t'el	이 근처 호텔

What is the address?
ju-so-ga ŏ-di-im-ni-kka?   주소가 어디입니까?
Would you write down the
address in Korean, please?
Han-guk-ŏ-ro ju-so jom jŏk-ŏ   한국어로 주소 좀 적어
ju-shi-gess-sŭm-ni-kka?   주시겠습니까?

At the Hotel
Checking in

I have a booking in the name of ...

... -i-rŭm-ŭ-ro ye-yak-haess-sŭm-ni-da　　...이름으로 예약했습니다

Do you have any rooms available?

bang iss-sŭm-ni-kka?　　방 있습니까?

I would like a ...	*... wŏn-ham-ni-da*	... 원합니다
Western-style single room	*yang-shik dok-bang*	양식 독방
Korean-style single room	*han-shik dok-bang*	한식 독방
single room	*dok-bang*	독방
shared room	*ham-kke sa-yong-hal bang*	함께 사용할 방
double room	*i-in-yong bang*	2인용 방
room with a private bathroom	*yok-shil-id-nŭn bang*	옥실있는 방
room with a shared bathroom	*kong-yong yok-shil-id-nŭn bang*	공용 옥실있는 방

I want a room with a/an ...	*... -bang-ŭ-ro ju-ship-shi-yo*	... 방으로 주십시오
air-conditioner	*e-ŏ-k'ŏn-i id-nŭn*	에어컨이 있는
bathroom	*yok-shil-i id-nŭn*	옥실이 있는
good view	*jŏn-mang-i jo-hŭn*	전망이 좋은
shower	*sya-wŏ-shil-i id-nŭn*	샤워실이 있는
telephone	*jŏn-hwa-ga id-nŭn*	전화가 있는
TV	*t'el-le-bi-jŏn-i id-nŭn*	텔레비전이 있는

| toilet | *hwa-jang-shil-i id-nŭn* | 화장실이 있는 |
| video | *bi-di-o-ga id-nŭn* | 비디오가 있는 |

How much is it (per night)/(per person)?
bang kap-shi (ha-ru-e)/(han sa-ram-dang) ŏl-ma-im-ni-kka? — 방 값이 (하루에)/(한 사람당) 얼마입니까?

Does the rate include the service charge?
sŏ-bi-sŭ-yo-gŭm-i p'o-ham doe-ŏss-sŭm-ni-kka? — 서비스요금이 포함 되었습니까?

Can I see the room?
bang-ŭl bol su iss-sum-ni-kka? — 방을 볼 수 있습니까?

Are there any others?
da-rŭn bang-i iss-sŭm-ni-kka? — 다른 방이 있습니까?

Do you have a ... room?
... -bang-i iss-sŭm-ni-kka? — ...방이 있습니까?

quieter	*dŏ jo-yong-han*	더 조용한
smaller	*dŏ ja-gŭn*	더 작은
larger	*dŏ k'ŭn*	더 큰
cheaper	*dŏ san*	더 싼

Can I see your price list?
yo-gŭm-p'yo-rŭl bo-yŏ ju-shi-gess-sŭm-ni-kka? — 요금표를 보여 주시겠습니까?

Is there a student discount?
hak-saeng hal-in-i iss-sŭm-ni-kka? — 학생 할인이 있습니까?

Do you allow children?
  a-i-dŭl-i mŏ-mul su iss-sŭm-ni-kka? 아이들이 머물 수 있습니까?

Is there a discount for children?
  a-i-dŭl hal-in-i doem-ni-kka? 아이들 할인이 됩니까?

Does it include breakfast?
  a-ch'im shik-sa-bi-ga p'o-ham-doe-ŏss-sŭm-ni-kka? 아침 식사비가 포함되었습니까?

It's fine. I'll take it.
  jo-sŭm-ni-da. mŏ-mul-gess-sŭm-ni-da 좋습니다. 머물겠습니다

Can I have a receipt?
  yŏng-su-jŭng-ŭl ju-shi-gess-sŭm-ni-kka? 영수증을 주시겠습니까?

I am going to stay   *... -man mŏ-mul-*   ...만 머물겠습니다
for ...   *gess-sŭm-ni-da*
  one day   *ha-ru*   하루
  two days   *i-t'ŭl*   이틀
  one week   *il ju-il*   일 주일

I'm not sure how long I'll be staying.
  ŏl-ma-dong-an mŏ-mul-ji mo-rŭ-gess-sŭm-ni-da 얼마동안 머물지 모르겠습니다

Where is the ...?   *... ŏ-di-e iss-sŭm-ni-kka?*   ...어디에 있습니까?
  bathroom   *yok-shil*   욕실
  toilet   *hwa-jang-shil*   화장실
  elevator   *el-li-be-i-t'ŏ*   엘리베이터
  kitchen   *bu-ŏk*   부엌

Can I use the kitchen?
*bu-ŏk-ŭl sa-yong-hal su iss-
sŭm-ni-kka?*
부엌을 사용할 수 있습니까?

Do I leave my key at reception?
*bang yŏl-soe-rŭl an-nae-shil-e
mat-gyŏ-ya ham-ni-kka?*
방 열쇠를 안내실에
맡겨야 합니까?

Is there hot water all day?
*dŏ-un mul-i ha-ru-jong-il na-
om-ni-kka?*
더운 물이 하루종일
나옵니까?

Requests

I wish to keep this in your safe.
*i-gŏ-sŭl bo-gwan-ham-e mat-
gi-go ship-sŭm-ni-da*
이것을 보관함에 맡기고
싶습니다

I wish to have my things from the safe.
*je-ga mat-gin kŏt jom ju-ship-
shi-yo*
제가 맡긴 것 좀 주십시오

Could you store this/these for me?
*i-kŏt/jŏ-gŏ-sŭl mat-gil su iss-
sŭm-ni-kka?*
이것/저것을 맡길 수 있습니까?

Could someone look after my child?
*a-i bo-nŭn sa-ram-ŭl ku-hae ju
-shil su iss-sŭm-ni-kka?*
아이 보는 사람을 구해 주실
수 있습니까?

Please wake me up at ... tomorrow.
*nae-il ... -shi-e kkae-wŏ ju-
ship-shi-yo*
내일 ...시에 깨워 주십시오

The room needs to be cleaned.
*bang chŏ'ng-so-hae ju-ship-
shi-yo*
방 청소해 주십시오

Please change my sheets.
ch'im-dae shi-t'ŭ-rŭl kal-a ju-ship-shi-yo   침대 시트를 갈아 주십시오

I would like room service please.
rum sŏ-bi-sŭ-rŭl bu-t'ak-ham-ni-da   룸 서비스를 부탁합니다

Please send breakfast to my room.
a-ch'im-shik-sa-rŭl bang-ŭ-ro kat-da ju-ship-shi-yo   아침식사를 방으로 갖다 주십시오

Is there someone who speaks English?
yŏng-ŏ t'ong-yŏk hal sa-ram-i iss-sŭm-ni-kka?   영어 통역 할 사람이 있습니까?

Complaints

I don't like this room.
bang-i mam-e an dŭ-rŏ-yo   방이 맘에 안 들어요

It's too small.
nŏ-mu jak-sŭm-ni-da   너무 작습니다

It's too (cold)/(hot).
nŏ-mu (ch'up)/(dŏp) sŭm-ni-da   너무 (춥)(덥)습니다

It's noisy.
shi-kkŭ-rŏp-sŭm-ni-da   시끄럽습니다

It's too dark.
nŏ-mu ŏ-dup-sŭm-ni-da   너무 어둡습니다

It smells.
naem-sae-ga nam-ni-da   냄새가 납니다

It's expensive.
bi-sam-ni-da   비쌉니다

I can't open the window.
ch'ang-mun-ŭl yŏl su ŏp-sŭm-ni-da   창문을 열 수 없습니다

I can't close the window.
ch'ang-mun-ŭl dat-ul su ŏb-sŭm-ni-da　　창문을 닫을 수 없습니다

The toilet won't flush.
byŏn-gi-ga ko-jang-nass-sŭm-ni-da　　변기가 고장났습니다

There is no electricity.
jŏn-gi-ga an dŭl-ŏ-om-ni-da　　전기가 안 들어옵니다

The ... does not work.	... *ko-jang-nass-sŭm-ni-da*	... 고장났습니다
air-conditioner	*e-ŏ-k'ŏn*	에어컨
heating	*nan-bang-jang-ch'i*	난방장치
lift	*el-li-be-i-t'ŏ*	엘리베이터
light	*jŏn-dŭng*	전등
shower	*sya-wŏ*	샤워
telephone	*jŏn-hwa*	전화
TV	*t'el-le-bi-jŏn*	텔레비전
toilet	*hwa-jang-shil*	화장실
video	*bi-di-o*	비디오

The shower won't drain properly.
sya-wŏ-jang-e mul-i an ppa-jim-ni-da　　샤워장에 물이 안 빠집니다

I have lost my ...	... *il-hŏ bŏ-ryŏss-sŭm-ni-da*	... 잃어 버렸습니다
bag	*ka-bang*	가방
key	*yŏl-soe*	열쇠
money	*don*	돈
passport	*yŏ-gwŏn*	여권

| travellers' cheques | *yŏ-haeng-ja su-p'yo* | 여행자 수표 |
| watch | *shi-gye* | 시계 |

Checking Out

I would like to check out ...	*... ttŏ-na-gess-sŭm-ni-da*	... 떠나겠습니다
now	*ji-kŭm*	지금
at noon	*jŏng-o-e*	정오에
tomorrow	*nae-il*	내일

I would like to pay my account.
kye-san ha-gess-sŭm-ni-da   계산 하겠습니다

Do you accept ...?	*... bat-sŭm-ni-kka?*	... 받습니까?
American Express	*A-me-ri-k'an ik-sŭ-p'ŭ-re-sŭ*	아메리칸 익스프레스
foreign currency	*oe-hwa*	외화
MasterCard	*Ma-sŭ-t'ŏ k'a-dŭ*	마스터 카드
travellers' cheques	*yŏ-haeng-ja su-p'yo*	여행자 수표
Visa	*Bi-ja k'a-dŭ*	비자 카드

There seems to be an error in my account.
kye-san-i jal-mot-doen kŏt   계산이 잘못된 것 같습니다
kass-sŭm-ni-da
Can I leave my luggage here?
jim-ŭl bo-gwan-hae ju-shi-   짐을 보관해 주시겠습니까?
gess-sŭm-ni-kka?

80 Laundry

I'm returning ...	... dol-a om-ni-da	... 돌아 옵니다
at 5 pm	o-hu da-sŏt-shi-e	오후 5시에
in a few days	myŏ-ch'il an-e	며칠 안에
tomorrow	nae-il	내일

Laundry

Please arrange dry-cleaning for me.
dŭ-ra-i-k'ŭ-ri-ning jom bu-t'ak-ham-ni-da
드라이크리닝 좀
부탁합니다

Is there somewhere to (wash)/(iron) clothes?
(se-t'ak)/(da-ri-mi jil) hal ko-shi iss-sŭm-ni-kka?
(세탁)/(다리미질)할 곳이
있습니까?

This washing isn't mine.
i se-t'ak-mul-ŭn je kŏt-i a-nim-ni-da
이 세탁물은 제 것이
아닙니다

Some Useful Words & Phrases

I have locked myself out of my room.
yŏl-soe-rŭl no-go mun-ŭl jam-gŭ-go na-wass-sŭm-ni-da
열쇠를 놓고 문을 잠그고
나왔습니다

Who is it?
nu-gu-shim-ni-kka?
누구십니까?

Just a minute.
jam-kkan-man ki-da-ri-ship-shi-yo
잠깐만 기다리십시오

Come in.
dŭl-ŏ o-ship-shi-yo
들어 오십시오

address	*ju-so*	주소
air-conditioned	*e-ŏ-k'ŏn*	에어컨
babysitter	*a-i bo-nŭn sa-ram*	아이 보는 사람
bathroom	*yok-shil*	욕실
bed	*ch'im-dae*	침대
blanket	*dam-yo*	담요
chair	*ŭi-ja*	의자
clean	*kkae-kkŭt-han*	깨끗한
cold	*ch'u-un*	추운
cot	*a-i ch'im-dae*	아이 침대
double bed	*dŏ-bŭl be-dŭ*	더블 베드
electricity	*jŏn-gi*	전기
fan	*sŏn-p'ung-gi*	선풍기
fax	*p'aek-sŭ*	팩스
hot	*ttŭ-gŏ-un*	뜨거운
key	*yŏl-soe*	열쇠
lift (elevator)	*el-li-be-i-t'ŏ*	엘리베이터
light bulb	*jŏn-gu*	전구
lock	*ja-mul-soe*	자물쇠
mattress	*yo*	요
message	*me-shi-ji*	메시지
pillow	*be-gae*	베개
pillowcase	*be-ge-it*	베개잇
room	*bang*	방
sheet	*shi-t'ŭ*	시트
shower	*sya-wŏ*	샤워

82 Some Useful Words & Phrases

soap	*bi-nu*	비누
suitcase	*ka-bang*	가방
swimming pool	*su-yŏng-jang*	수영장
table	*t'e-i-bŭl*	테이블
toilet	*hwa-jang-shil*	화장실
toilet paper	*hwa-jang-ji*	화장지
towel	*su-gŏn*	수건
water	*mul*	물
cold water	*naeng-su*	냉수
hot water	*on-su*	온수
drinking water	*ŭm-ryo-su*	음료수
window	*ch'ang-mun*	창문

Around Town

The two largest cities in Korea are Seoul (the capital) and Pusan (South Korea's principal port). The cities are very modern and have well-developed public transport systems. However, as both cities are densely populated and very busy, the transport services are often pushed beyond their capacities. This frequent congestion also occurs with pedestrians. In some parts of these cities, you don't need to walk – just flow with the crowd!

The best way to see Seoul, and the other major cities, is on foot. Use the buses or subway to get to particular areas of interest. There is a plethora of tourist maps and information about Korean culture, history and places of interest available from the Korea National Tourism Corporation.

Outside the cities, life is relatively less intense. For those with limited time in Korea, there are many organised tours available with English-speaking guides.

Can you direct me to ...?	... -e ka-nŭn kil-ŭl al-lyŏ ju-ship-shi-yo?	...에 가는 길을 알려 주십시오?
I'm looking for ...	... ch'at-go iss-sŭm-ni-da	... 찾고 있습니다
the art gallery	hwa-rang	화랑
a bank	ŭn-haeng	은행
the central post office	jung-ang-u-ch'e-guk	중앙우체국
a church	kyo-hoe	교회
the city centre	shi-nae-jung-shim-ga	시내중심가

the ... embassy	... dae-sa-gwan	... 대사관
my hotel	ho-t'el	호텔
the market	shi-jang	시장
the museum	bak-mul-gwan	박물관
the police station	kyŏng-ch'al-sŏ	경찰서
the post office	u-ch'e-guk	우체국
a public telephone	kong-jung-jŏn-hwa	공중전화
a public toilet	hwa-jang-shil	화장실
a restaurant	re-sŭ-t'o-rang	레스토랑
the tourist infor- mation office	kwan-gwang-an- nae-so	관광안내소

Please write down the directions
in Korean.
    han-guk-ŏ-ro yak-do jom kŭ-   한국어로 약도 좀 그려
    ryŏ ju-ship-shi-yo   주십시오
What time does it open?
    myŏt shi-e mun-i yŏl-lim-   몇 시에 문이 열립니까?
    ni-kka?
What time does it close?
    myŏt shi-e mun-ŭl das-sŭm-   몇 시에 문을 닫습니까?
    ni-kka?

For directions, see Getting Around , page 52.

At the Bank

Banks that exchange foreign currency and travellers' cheques
have a `Foreign Exchange' sign displayed outside. You must have
your passport to exchange money. Keep the exchange receipts,
as you will need them when exchanging Korean currency before
leaving the country. When travelling outside cities, make sure you

have enough Korean currency, as there may not be an exchange bank in some areas. If you take cash to Korea, US currency is the most widely accepted.

Where can I exchange some ...?	*... ŏ-di-sŏ ba-kkul su iss-sŭm-ni-kka?*	... 어디서 바꿀 수 있습니까?
travellers' cheques	*yŏ-haeng-ja su-p'yo*	여행자 수표
foreign currency	*oe-hwa*	외화

I want to exchange some money.
oe-hwa-rŭl ba-kku-go ship-sŭm-ni-da 외화를 바꾸고 싶습니다

What is the exchange rate?
dal-lŏ-ŭi hwan-yul-i ŏl-ma-im-ni-kka? 달러의 환율이 얼마입니까?

How many Korean won per ... dollar?
... dal-la-dang myŏt wŏn-im-ni-kka? ... 달라당 몇 원입니까?

Can I have money transferred here from my bank?
je ŭn-haeng ku-jwa-e-sŏ i ŭn-haeng-ŭ-ro don-ŭl song-gŭm-hal su iss-sŭm-ni-kka? 제 은행 구좌에서 이 은행으로 돈을 송금할 수 있습니까?

How long will it take to arrive?
do-ch'ak-ha-nŭn-de ŏl-ma-na kŏl-lim-ni-kka? 도착하는데 얼마나 걸립니까?

Has my money arrived yet?
don-i do-ch'ak doe-ŏss-sŭm-ni-kka? 돈이 도착 되었습니까?

I'm expecting some money
from ...
   ... -e-sŏ don-i ol ye-jŏng-im-   ... 에서 돈이 올 예정입니다
   ni-da
Where do I sign?
   ŏ-di-e sŏ-myŏng-ŭl ham-   어디에 서명을 합니까?
   ni-kka?

Some Useful Words

bankdraft	*ŭn-haeng ŏ-ŭm*	은행 어음
banknotes	*ŭn-haeng-gwŏn*	은행권
cash	*hyŏn-gŭm*	현금
cashier	*ch'ul-nap-wŏn*	출납원
coins	*dong-jŏn*	동전
credit card	*shin-yong k'a-dŭ*	신용 카드
exchange rate	*hwan-yul*	환율
notes	*ji-p'ye*	지폐
passport	*yŏ-gwŏn*	여권
signature	*sŏ-myŏng*	서명
travellers' cheques	*yŏ-haeng-ja su-p'yo*	여행자 수표

At the Post Office

Postal charges are relatively inexpensive in Korea. Seoul Central
Post Office provides a fast, inexpensive, quality overseas goods
packing service. It's a great way to send things home.

Where is the ...?   *... ŏ-di-e iss-sŭm-ni-*   ... 어디에 있습니까?
   kka?

post office	*u-ch'e-guk*	우체국
central post office	*jung-ang u-ch'e-guk*	중앙 우체국

AROUND TOWN

I would like to send ...	... *bo-nae-go ship-sŭm-ni-da*	... 보내고 싶습니다
a fax	*p'aek-sŭ*	팩스
a letter	*p'yŏn-ji*	편지
a parcel	*so-p'o*	소포
a postcard	*yŏp-sŏ*	엽서
a registered letter	*dŭng-gi-u-p'yŏn*	등기우편

| by air | *hang-gong-p'yŏn-ŭ-ro* | 항공편으로 |
| by sea | *sŏn-bak-p'yŏn-ŭ-ro* | 선박편으로 |

I would like to buy ...	... *sa-go ship-sŭm-ni-da*	... 사고 싶습니다
some stamps	*u-p'yo*	우표
some aerograms	*e-ŏ-ro-gŭ-raem*	에어로그램

How much is the postage?
u-p'yŏn yo-gŭm-i ŏl-ma-im-ni-kka?

우편 요금이 얼마입니까?

Where can I get these packed?
p'o-jang-ha-nŭn ko-shi ŏ-di-e iss-sŭm-ni-kka?

포장하는 곳이 어디에 있습니까?

How much does it cost to pack these?
p'o-jang-ryo-ga ŏl-ma-im-ni-kka?

포장료가 얼마입니까?

Some Useful Words

address	*ju-so*	주소
aerogram	*e-ŏ-ro-gŭ-raem*	에어로그램
airmail	*hang-gong u-p'yŏn*	항공 우편

AROUND TOWN

envelope	*bong-t'u*	봉투
mailbox	*u-ch'e-t'ong*	우체통
packing service	*p'o-jang*	포장
parcel	*so-p'o*	소포
registered mail	*dŭng-gi*	등기
stamp	*u-p'yo*	우표
surface mail	*bo-t'ong u-p'yŏn*	보통 우편

Telephone

Korea has both coin and card-operated telephones. Local calls are limited to three minutes, but can be extended by inserting additional coins. They do not provide change or refunds but any remaining credit can be used for additional three minute calls.

As long-distance calls are time-charged and you have to maintain a credit, it is preferable to use card-operated phones for long-distance calls.

Phone cards may be purchased from banks, shops near card-operated phones and 24-hour convenience stores. There is a 30% discount on calls made between 9 pm and 8 am, Monday to Saturday and all day on Sundays and public holidays.

Hello, I want to call ...
yŏ-bo-se-yo, ... jŏn-hwa jom bu-t'ak-ham-ni-da

여보세요, ... 전화 좀 부탁합니다

The number is ...
jŏn-hwa bŏn-ho-nŭn ... im-ni-da

전화 번호는 ... 입니다

I want to speak for three minutes.
sam-bun-dong-an t'ong-hwa-ha-go ship-sum-ni-da

3분동안 통화하고 싶습니다

How much does a three-minute call cost?
sam-bun t'ong-hwa-ryo-ga ŏl-ma-im-ni-kka?

3분 통화료가 얼마입니까?

How much does each extra minute cost?
il-bun ch'u-ga t'ong-hwa-ryo-nŭn ŏl-ma-im-ni-kka?

1분 추가 통화료는 얼마입니까?

I want to make a reverse charges phone call.
k'ol-laek-t'ŭ-k'ol-ŭl bu-t'ak-ham-ni-da

콜랙트콜을 부탁합니다

I would like speak to ...
...-ha-go t'ong-hwa-ha-go ship-sŭm-ni-da

... 하고 통화하고 싶습니다

Do you speak English?
Yŏng-ŏ-rŭl ha-shim-ni-kka?

영어를 하십니까?

Yes, he/she is here.
ne, kye-shim-ni-da

네, 계십니다

One moment, please.
jam-kkan-man, ki-da-ri-ship-shi-yo

잠깐만 기다리십시오

Operator, I've been cut off.
yŏ-bo-se-yo, jŏn-hwa-ga kkŭn-ŏ-jyŏss-sŭm-ni-da

여보세요, 전화가
끊어졌습니다

Please call again for me.
da-shi jŏn-hwa-rŭl bu-t'ak-ham-ni-da

다시 전화를 부탁합니다

Is there a direct dial line?
di-di-di-ga doem-ni-kka?

디디디가 됩니까?

How do I get an outside line?
oe-bu-ro jŏn-hwa-rŭl ŏ-ttŏ-ke ham-ni-kka?

외부로 전화를
어떻게 합니까?

Excuse me, please, can you speak slowly?
shil-lye-ji-man, ch'ŏn-ch'ŏn-hi mal-sŭm-hae ju-shi-gess-sŭm-ni-kka?

실례지만, 천천히 말씀해
주시겠습니까?

Please ask him/her to call me on ...
... -han-t'e jŏn-hwa-hae dal-la-go jŏn-hae-ju-ship-shi-yo

... 한테 전화해 달라고
전해주십시오

I'll ring again ...	*... jŏn-hwa da-shi ha-gess-sŭm-ni-da*	... 전화 다시 하겠습니다
later	*na-jung-e*	나중에
tomorrow	*nae-il*	내일
tonight	*o-nŭl-bam*	오늘밤

Thank you. Goodbye.
kam-sa-ham-ni-da. an-nyŏng-hi kye-ship-shi-yo

감사합니다 안녕히
계십시오

AROUND TOWN

Some Useful Words

area code	*ji-yŏk bŏn-ho*	지역 번호
direct dial	*ja-dong jŏn-hwa*	자동 전화
engaged	*t'ong-hwa-jung*	통화중
an international call	*kuk-je jŏn-hwa*	국제 전화
a local call	*shi-nae jŏn-hwa*	시내 전화
a long-distance call	*shi-oe jŏn-hwa*	시외 전화
person to person	*t'ŭk-jŏng-in ho-ch'ul-jŏn-hwa*	특정인 호출전화
public telephone	*kong-jung jŏn-hwa*	공중 전화
reverse charges	*k'ol-laek-t'ŭ-k'ol*	콜렉트콜
telephone	*jŏn-hwa*	전화
telephone booth	*jŏn-hwa bak-sŭ*	전화 박스
telephone card	*jŏn-hwa k'a-dŭ*	전화 카드
telephone charges	*jŏn-hwa yo-gŭm*	전화 요금
telephone number	*jŏn-hwa bŏn-ho*	전화 번호

Sightseeing

Where is the nearest tourist information centre?

i kŭn-ch'ŏ kwan-gwang-an-nae-so-ga ŏ-di-e iss-sŭm-ni-kka?

이 근처 관광안내소가 어디에 있습니까?

Do you have a local map in English?

yŏng-ŏ shi-nae ji-do-ga iss-sŭm-ni-kka?

영어 시내 지도가 있습니까?

Can I take photographs?

sa-jin jom jjik-ŏ-do doem-ni-kka?

사진 좀 찍어도 됩니까?

Could you take a photograph
of me?
   sa-jin jom jjik-ŏ ju-shi-gess-   사진 좀 찍어 주시겠습니까?
   sŭm-ni-kka?

Where are the interesting places
in this area?
   i kŭn-ch'ŏ-e kwan-gwang-hal   이 근처에 관광할 곳이
   ko-shi ŏ-di-im-ni-kka?   어디입니까?

What's this ...?	*i ... mu-ŏt-im-ni-kka?*	이 ... 무엇입니까?
building	*kŏn-mul*	건물
market	*shi-jang*	시장
monument	*ki-nyŏm-bi*	기념비
palace	*kung-jŏn*	궁전

How old is it?
   ŏl-ma-na o-rae doe-ŏss-sŭm-   얼마나 오래 되었습니까?
   ni-kka?

Who lived there?   누가 살았습니까?
   nu-ga sal-ass-sŭm-ni-kka?

Who was the ...?	*... nu-ku-yŏss-sŭm-ni-kka?*	... 누구였습니까?
architect	*kŏn-ch'uk-ga*	건축가
artist	*hwa-ga*	화가

Do you have tours to ...?	*... kwan-gwang-i iss-sŭm-ni-kka?*	... 관광이 있습니까?
Cheju Island	*Je-ju-do*	제주도

the Korean Folk Village	*min-sok-ch'on*	민속촌
Kyŏngju	*Kyŏng-ju*	경주
Mt. Sorak National Park	*Sŏl-ak-san*	설악산
P'anmunjŏm	*P'an-mun-jŏm*	판문점
the Olympic Stadium	*Sŏl-ul-jong-hap-un-dong-jang*	서울종합운동장

Do you have English-speaking guides?
Yŏng-ŏ-rŭl ha-nŭn an-nae-wŏn-i iss-sŭm-ni-kka?

영어를 하는 안내원이 있습니까?

How much does it cost?
ŏl-ma-im-ni-kka?

얼마입니까?

What time does it leave?
myŏt shi-e ttŏ-nam-ni-kka?

몇 시에 떠납니까?

How long is the tour?
kwan-gwang-ha-nŭn-de ŏl-ma-na kŏl-lim-ni-kka?

관광하는데 얼마나 걸립니까?

Do you pick up from my/our hotel?
ho-t'el-lo de-ri-ryŏ om-ni-kka?

호텔로 데리려 옵니까?

Where does the bus leave from?
ŏ-di-e-sŏ bŏ-sŭ-ga ttŏ-nam-ni-kka?

어디에서 버스가 떠납니까?

Places of Interest in Seoul

casino	*k'a-ji-no*	카지노
Ch'angdŏk Palace	*Ch'ang-dŏk-gung*	창덕궁
Ch'anggyŏng Palace	*Ch'ang-gyŏng-gung*	창경궁
Han River cruise	*Han-hang yu-ram-sŏn*	한강 유람선
Itaewon	*I-t'ae-wŏn*	이태원
Kimch'i Museum of Korea	*kim-ch'i bak-mul-gwan*	김치 박물관
Kyŏngbok Palace	*Kyŏng-bok-gung*	경복궁
Kyŏnghŭi Palace	*Kyŏng-hŭi-gung*	경희궁
Lotte World	*Rot-de wŏl-dŭ*	롯데 월드
Mt. Nam Park	*Nam-san*	남산
Myŏng-dong	*Myŏng-dong*	명동
National Theatre	*kuk-rip kŭk-jang*	국립 극장
the Olympic Park	*Ol-lim-p'ik kong-wŏn*	올림픽 공원
the Olympic Stadium	*Sŏ-ul jong-hap-un-dong-jang*	서울 종합운동장
Pagoda Park	*P'a-go-da kong-wŏn*	파고다 공원
Pongun Temple	*Bong-un-sa*	봉운사
Poshin-gak Pavillion	*Bo-shin-gak*	보신각
Sejong Culture Centre	*Se-jong mun-hwa-hoe-gwan*	세종 문화회관
Seoul Grand Park	*Sŏ-ul dae-gong-wŏn*	서울 대공원
Seoul National Museum	*kuk-rip jung-ang-bak-mul-gwan*	국립 중앙박물관

AROUND TOWN

Seoul Nori Madang	*Sŏ-ul no-ri-ma-dang*	서울 놀이마당
South Gate	*Nam-dae-mun*	남대문
Tŏksu Palace	*Dŏk-su-gung*	덕수궁
Yŏŭido	*Yŏ-ŭi-do*	여의도

Places of Interest in Pusan

Chagalch'i Fish Market	*Ja-gal-ch'i shi-jang*	자갈치 시장
Haeundae	*Hae-un-dae*	해운대
Mt. Kŭmjŏng	*Kŭm-jŏng san-sŏng*	금정 산성
Pŏmŏ Temple	*Bŏm-ŏ-sa*	범어사
Pusan Tower	*Bu-san t'a-wŏ*	부산 타워
Taejongdae	*T'ae-jong-dae*	태종대
UN Cemetery	*Yu-En kuk-rim-myo-ji*	유엔 국립묘지

Some Useful Words

ancient	*yet-nal-ui*	옛날의
Buddhist temples	*jŏl*	절
cathedral	*dae-sŏng-dang*	대성당
kiosk	*mae-jŏm*	매점
national parks	*kuk-rip kong-wŏn*	국립 공원
old city	*yet-do-shi*	옛도시
pagoda	*p'a-go-da*	파고다

Royal Palace	*kung-jŏng*	궁정
statues	*dong-sang*	동상
university	*dae-hak-gyo*	대학교
zoo	*dong-mul-wŏn*	동물원

AROUND TOWN

Nightlife

In the larger cities, you will find discotheques, nightclubs, theatre restaurants, beer halls, cinemas, theatres and karaoke bars. These close at midnight due to government regulations.

It is well worth the money to see Korean traditional dance and music performances.

Western entertainment, food and drinks are generally more expensive than Korean food and drinks. If you are a budget traveller, nightclubs and beer halls at luxury hotels are not recommended.

What is there to do in the
evening?
    jŏ-nyŏk-e hal su it-nŭn ko-shi   저녁에 할 수 있는 것이
    mu-ŏt-im-ni-kka?   무엇입니까?

How much does it cost to get in?
    ip-jang-ryo-ga ŏl-ma im-   입장료가 얼마 입니까?
    ni-kka?

I would like to see ...	... *bo-go ship-sŭm-ni-da*	... 보고 싶습니다
the city at night	*shi-nae ya-kyŏng*	시내 야경
a Korean movie	*Han-guk yŏng-hwa*	한국 영화

Is there an inexpensive ...?
    ... *san ko-shi iss-sŭm-ni-kka?*   ... 싼 곳이 있습니까?

AROUND TOWN

Can you recommend a good ...?	jo-hŭn ... so-gae-hae ju-shi-gess-sŭm-ni-kka?	좋은... 소개해 주시겠습니까?
beer hall	maek-ju-jip	맥주집
disco	di-sŭ-k'o-jang	디스코장
karaoke bar	no-rae-bang	노래방
Korean wine bar	sul-jip	술집
local theatre	kŭk-jang	극장
nightclub	na-i-t'ŭ-k'ŭl-lŏp	나이트클럽

I am interested in Korean ...	Han-guk ...-e kwan-shim iss-sŭm-ni-da	한국... 에 관심 있습니다
dramatic song	p'an-so-ri	판소리
drum dance	jang-ku-ch'um	장구춤
mask dance	t'al-ch'um	탈춤
monk's dance	sŭng-mu	승무
music and dance	kuk-ak-gwa ko-jŏn-mu-yong	국악과 고전무용
six-string zither	kŏ-mun-go	거문고
twelve-string zither	ka-ya-gŭm	가야금

six-string zither

Where can I buy a ticket?
p'yo-rŭl ŏ-de-sŏ sam-ni-kka?　　표를 어디서 삽니까?

I'd like to buy ... ticket(s) please.
...-p'yo-rŭl sa-go ship-sŭm-ni-da　　... 표를 사고 싶습니다

Do they have Korean food?
han-shik-i iss-sŭm-ni-kka?　　한식이 있습니까?

What clothes should I wear?
mu-sŭn o-sŭl i-pŏ-ya ham-ni-kka?　　무슨 옷을 입어야 합니까?

Do I have to book?
ye-yak-hae-ya ham-ni-kka?　　예약해야 합니까?

What time do they open?
myŏt shi-e yŏl-lim-ni-kka?　　몇 시에 열립니까?

Some Useful Words

ballet	*bal-le*	발레
billiard hall	*dang-gu-jang*	당구장
cinema	*yŏng-hwa*	영화
concert	*yŏn-ju-hoe*	연주회
opera	*o-p'e-ra*	오페라
stadium	*kyŏng-gi-jang*	경기장
tennis court	*t'e-ni-sŭ-jang*	테니스장

In the Country

If you travel in country areas, you will discover a way of life which is less hectic than the cities and much closer to the traditional Korean lifestyle. You will, however, meet fewer people who can speak English.

It is possible to reach most areas in Korea by some form of public transport, and most places of interest have international standard tourist facilities. For a real cultural experience, try staying in yŏgwans in the smaller cities and towns.

Korea has much mountainous and rugged terrain, especially on the east coast. There are about 20 national parks and many have waterways, mountains and even Buddhist temples.

Places to visit include Mt Sŏrak (skiing in winter), P'anmunjŏm (Peace Village in the Demilitarized Zone), Puyo (Paekje Kingdom tombs and artefacts), Kwangju (site of the people's uprising), Kyŏngju (Shilla Kingdom tombs and artefacts), Cheju Island (subtropical island approximately 85 km south of the peninsula), and the islands and waterways along the southern coasts of the peninsula.

Weather

What's the weather like?
nal-shi-ga ŏ-ttŏ-sŭm-ni-kka?   날씨가 어떻습니까?

The weather is ...   *o-nŭl nal-shi-ga ...*   오늘 날씨가 ...
today.
    cold   *ch'up-sŭm-ni-da*   춥습니다
    cool   *shi-wŏn-ham-ni-da*   시원합니다

fine	jo-sŭm-ni-da	좋습니다
freezing	mop-shi ch'up-sŭm-ni-da	몹시 춥습니다
hot	dŏp-sŭm-ni-da	덥습니다
very humid	mu-dŏp-sŭm-ni-da	무덥습니다
warm	tta-ttŭt-ham-ni-da	따뜻합니다

Will it be ... tomorrow?	nae-il nal-shi-ga ...-gŏt kas-sŭm-ni-kka?	내일 날씨가 ...것 같습니까?
cloudy	hŭ-ril	흐릴
raining	bi ol	비 올
snowing	nun ol	눈 올
sunny	mal-gŭl	맑을
windy	ba-ram bul	바람 불

IN THE COUNTRY

Some Useful Words

average temperature	p'yŏng-gyun on-do	평균 온도
cloud	ku-rŭm	구름
drizzle	i-sŭl-bi	이슬비
drought	ka-mum	가뭄

fog	*an-gae*	안개
frost	*sŏ-ri*	서리
ice	*ŏl-ŭm*	얼음
lightning	*bŏn-gae*	번개
mud	*jin-hŭg*	진흙
rain	*bi*	비
rainbow	*mu-ji-gae*	무지개
the rainy season	*jang-ma-ch'ŏl*	장마철
snow	*nun*	눈
storm	*p'ok-p'ung*	폭풍
sun	*t'ae-yang*	태양
thunder	*ch'ŏn-dung*	천동
thunderstorm	*noe-u*	뇌우
weather	*nal-shi*	날씨
weather forecast	*il-gi-ye-bo*	일기예보
wind	*ba-ram*	바람

Geographical Terms

agriculture	*nong-ŏp*	농업
beach	*hae-byŏn*	해변
bridge	*da-ri*	다리
cave	*dong-gul*	동굴
city	*do-shi*	도시
coast	*hae-an*	해안
country	*shi-gol*	시골
Earth	*ji-gu*	지구
earthquake	*ji-jin*	지진
farm	*nong-jang*	농장
forest	*sup*	숲
harbour	*hang-gu*	항구
hill	*ŏn-dŏk*	언덕

hot spring	*on-ch'ŏn*	온천
island	*sŏm*	섬
lake	*ho-su*	호수
map	*ji-do*	지도
mountain	*san*	산
mountain range	*san-maek*	산맥
national park	*kuk-rip-gong-wŏn*	국립공원
ocean	*dae-yang*	대양
ricefield	*non*	논
river	*kang*	강
scenery	*p'ung-gyŏng*	풍경
tide	*jo-su*	조수
valley	*san-gol-jjak*	산골짝
village	*ma-ŭl*	마을
walking track	*bo-do*	보도
waterfall	*p'ok-p'o*	폭포

IN THE COUNTRY

Animals

cat	*ko-yang-i*	고양이
cow	*am-so*	암소
deer	*sa-sŭm*	사슴
dog	*kae*	개
domestic animal	*ka-ch'uk*	가축
fish	*mul-go-gi*	물고기
frog	*kae-gu-ri*	개구리
goat	*yŏm-so*	염소
horse	*mal*	말
kangaroo	*k'aeng-g ŏ-ru*	캥거루
monkey	*wŏn-sung-i*	원숭이
ox	*hwang-so*	황소
pig	*dwae-ji*	돼지

rabbit	*t'o-kki*	토끼
rat	*jwi*	쥐
sheep	*yang*	양
snake	*baem*	뱀
spider	*kŏ-mi*	거미
tiger	*ho-rang-i*	호랑이
wild animal	*dŭl-jim-sŭng*	들짐승

Birds

bird	*sae*	새
canary	*k'a-na-ri-a*	카나리아
chicken	*dag*	닭
crow	*kka-ma-gwi*	까마귀
duck	*o-ri*	오리
eagle	*dok-su-ri*	독수리
goose	*kŏ-wi*	거위
hawk	*mae*	매
owl	*bu-ŏng-i*	부엉이
peacock	*kong-jak*	공작
pheasant	*kkwŏng*	꿩
pigeon	*bi-dul-gi*	비둘기
robin	*ul-sae*	울새
sparrow	*ch'am-sae*	참새

swan	*baek-jo*	백조
turkey	*ch'il-myŏn-jo*	칠면조
waterfowl	*mul-sae*	물새
wild duck	*dŭl-o-ri*	들오리
wild goose	*ki-rŏ-gi*	기러기

Insects

ant	*kae-mi*	개미
bee	*bŏl*	벌
butterfly	*na-bi*	나비
cicada	*mae-mi*	매미
firefly	*ban-dit-bul*	반딧불
fly	*p'a-ri*	파리
leech	*kŏ-mŏ-ri*	거머리
lice	*i*	이
mosquito	*mo-gi*	모기
silkworm	*nu-e*	누에

Plants

| carnation | *k'a-ne-i-syŏn* | 카네이션 |
| cherry blossom | *bŏt-kkot* | 벚꽃 |

chrysanthemum	*kuk-hwa*	국화
flower	*kkot*	꽃
hibiscus	*mu-gung-hwa*	무궁화
leaf	*ip*	잎
lily	*baek-hap*	백합
maple	*dan-p'ung-na-mu*	단풍나무
oak	*ch'am-na-mu*	참나무
orchid	*nan-ch'o*	난초
pine tree	*so-na-mu*	소나무
rose	*jang-mi*	장미
sunflower	*hae-ba-ra-gi*	해바라기
tree	*na-mu*	나무
vegetation	*ch'ae-so*	채소
violet	*je-bi-kkot*	제비꽃
water lily	*yŏn-kkot*	연꽃

Camping

There are a limited number of camp sites in Korea. You may camp on private land, but get permission from the owner first. Korea has a problem with water pollution, even in country areas, so check whether the water is safe to drink.

Am I allowed to camp here?
yŏ-gi-sŏ k'aem-p'ŭ-hae-do doe-gess-sŭm-ni-kka?
여기서 캠프해도 되겠습니까?

Is there a camp site nearby?
i kŭn-ch'ŏ-e k'aem-p'ŭ-jang-i iss-sŭm-ni-kka?
이 근처에 캠프장이 있습니까?

I want to hire a tent.
t'en-t'ŭ-rŭl bil-lil su iss-sŭm-ni-da
텐트를 빌릴 수 있습니까

Is it waterproof?
bang-su-ga doem-ni-kka?
방수가 됩니까?

Is there any drinking water?
shik-su-ga iss-sŭm-ni-kka?
식수가 있습니까?

Is this water safe to drink?
i mul-ŭl ma-shil su iss-sŭm-ni-kka?
이 물을 마실 수 있습니까?

Are there any ...? *... iss-sŭm ni-kka?* ... 있습니까?
shopping facilities	*mae-jŏm*	매점
showers/baths	*sya-wŏ-jang/yok-shil*	샤워장/욕실
toilets	*hwa-jang-shil*	화장실

Some Useful Words & Phrases

Where are we on this map?
u-ri-ga i ji-do-e-sŏ ŏ-di-e iss-sŭm-ni-kka?
우리가 이 지도에서 어디에 있습니까?

Please tell me how to get to ...
...-e ŏ-ttŏ-ke ka-nŭn-ji al-lyŏ-ju-ship-shi-yo
... 에 어떻게 가는지 알려주십시오

How far is it to ...?
... kka-ji ŏl-ma-na kŏl-lim-ni-kka?
... 까지 얼마나 걸립니까?

Is there anything to see here?
yŏ-gi-e ku-gyŏng-hal kŏ-shi iss-sŭm-ni-kka?
여기에 구경할 것이 있습니까?

Can I get there on foot?
kŏl-ŏ-sŏ kal su iss-sŭm-ni-kka?
걸어서 갈 수 있습니까?

Do I need a guide?
an-nae-wŏn-i iss-ŏ-ya ham-ni-kka?
안내원이 있어야 합니까?

Can I swim here?
su-yŏng-hae-do doem-ni-kka?
수영해도 됩니까?

What's that animal called?
i dong-mul-i-rŭm-i mu-ŏt-im-ni-kka?
이 동물이름이 무엇입니까?

What's that plant called?
i shik-mul-i-rŭm-i mu-ŏt-im-ni-kka?
이 식물이름이 무엇입니까?

Is there a ... near here?
i kŭn-ch'ŏ-e ... iss-sŭm-ni-kka?
이 근처에 ... 있습니까?

| north | buk-jjok | 북쪽 |
| south | nam-jjok | 남쪽 |

IN THE COUNTRY

east	*dong-jjok*	동쪽
west	*sŏ-jjok*	서쪽
backpack	*bae-nang*	배낭
butane gas	*bu-t'an ka-sŭ*	부탄 가스
camp bed	*jŏp-nŭn ch'im-dae*	접는 침대
camping equipment	*k'aem-p'ing jang-bi*	캠핑 장비
can opener	*kkang-t'ong tta-gae*	깡통 따개
candles	*yang-ch'o*	양초
compass	*na-ch'im-p'an*	나침판
fishing tackle	*nag-shi do-gu*	낚시 도구
fork	*p'o-k'ŭ*	포크
frying pan	*p'ŭ-ra-i-p'aen*	프라이팬
hammer	*mang-ch'i*	망치
hiking	*ha-i-k'ing*	하이킹
insect repellent	*bang-ch'ung-je*	방충제
knife	*k'al*	칼
matches	*sŏng-nyang*	성냥
mattress	*mae-t'ŭ-ri-sŭ*	매트리스
mosquito net	*mo-gi-jang*	모기장
mug	*ch'at-jan*	찻잔
plate	*jŏp-shi*	접시
pocket knife	*ju-mŏ-ni-k'al*	주머니칼
rope	*bat-jul*	밧줄
saucepan	*naem-bi*	냄비
sleeping bag	*ch'im-nang*	침낭
spoon	*sut-ga-rak*	숟가락
stove	*nan-ro*	난로
tent	*ch'ŏn-mak*	천막
tent pegs	*ch'ŏn-mak mal-ttuk*	천막 말뚝

IN THE COUNTRY

tent poles	*ch'ŏn-mak ki-dung*	천막 기둥
torch	*son jŏn-dŭng*	손 전등
vacuum flask	*bo-on-byŏng*	보온병
water bottle	*mul-byŏng*	물병

IN THE COUNTRY

Food

People who like to try different foods and who enjoy Asian food will have a wonderful time in Korea. If you can't stand garlic or hot spices you are also catered for, but be aware that Western meals are generally more expensive than Korean dishes.

There are five main types of cuisine available – Korean, Chinese, Japanese, Western and fast food. Korean and Chinese meals are the best value and the most popular. Many Korean dishes contain garlic, hot chilli, salt, sesame seeds, oil and soy sauce. Each region has its own specialities.

In traditional Korean restaurants you will be required to remove your shoes and sit on cushions on the floor. Korea has its own dining etiquette. For instance, it is perfectly acceptable and even considered as appreciative of the meal to make slurping sounds when eating. Do not, however, stick your chopsticks upright into the rice as this is considered a sign of death by Koreans.

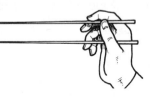

restaurant
   re-sŭ-t'o-rang   레스토랑
I am hungry.
   bae-ga ko-p'ŭm-ni-da   배가 고픕니다

I want something to ...	... ship-sŭm-ni-da	... 싶습니다
eat	mŏk-go	먹고
drink	ma-shi-go	마시고

Let's have ...	... mŏk-ŭp-shi-da	... 먹읍시다
breakfast	a-ch'im	아침
lunch	jŏm-shim	점심
dinner	jŏ-nyŏk	저녁

Can you suggest a good restaurant?
jo-hŭn ŭm-shik-jŏm-ŭl so-gae-hae ju-shi-gess-sŭm-ni-kka? 좋은 음식점을 소개해 주시겠습니까?

I would like to go to a ... restaurant	... re-sŭ-t'o-rang-e ka-go ship-sŭm-ni-da	... 레스토랑에 가고 싶습니다
bulgogi (beef)	bul-go-gi-jip	불고기집
cheap	san	싼
Chinese	Jung-guk ŭm-shik-jŏm	중국 음식점
dumpling	man-du-jip	만두집
Japanese	Il-shik-jip	일식집
Korean	Han-shik-jŏm	한식점
noodle	kuk-su-jip	국수집
Western	yang-shik-jŏm	양식점

food stall	ŭm-shik ka-ge	음식 가게
snack corner	kan-i-shik-dang	간이식당
steak house	sŭ-t'e-i-k'ŭ-jip	스테이크집
tearoom	da-bang	다방

At the Restaurant

Do you have a table for ...
persons, please?
...-myŏng ja-ri iss-sŭm-ni-kka?

...명 자리 있습니까?

Do you have a set menu?
jŏng-shik-i iss-sŭm-ni-kka?

정식이 있습니까?

What is the price per person?
il-in-dang ŏl-ma-im-ni-kka?

일인당 얼마입니까?

What does it include?
mu-ŏt-i na-om-ni-kka?

무엇이 나옵니까?

Hello. Waiter!
yŏ-bo-se-yo. we-i-t'ŏ!

여보세요. 웨이터!

Can I see the menu please?
*me-nyu jom ju-shi-gess-sŭm-
ni-kka?*

메뉴 좀 주시겠습니까?

Do you have a menu in English?
*Yŏng-ŏ-ro doen me-nyu-ga iss-
sŭm-ni-kka?*

영어로 된 메뉴가 있습니까?

What is your special dish today?
*o-nŭl t'ŭk-byŏl-yo-ri-ga mu-ŏt-
im-ni-kka?*

오늘 특별요리가
무엇입니까?

I would like the set lunch, please.
*jŏm-shim jŏng-shik-ŭ-ro ju-
ship-shi-yo*

점심 정식으로 주십시오

Can you serve me straight away?
ppal-li ju-shi-gess-sŭm-ni-kka?

빨리 주시겠습니까?

What is this/that?
*i-gŏt-i/jŏ-gŏt-i mu-ŏt-im-
ni-kka?*

이것이/저것이 무엇입니까?

I would like ...
... jom ju-ship-shi-yo
... 좀 주십시오

I'd like what s/he is having.
jŏ bun kŏt-gwa kat-ŭn kŏt-ŭ-ro ju-ship-shi-yo
저 분 것과 같은 것으로 주십시오

Another ..., please.
... ha-na dŏ ju-ship-shi-yo
... 하나 더 주십시오

Anything else?
da-rŭn kŏt-ŭl dŏ dŭ-ril-kka-yo?
다른 것을 더 드릴까요?

Not too spicy please.
nŏ-mu maep-ji an-nŭn kŏt-ŭ-ro ju-ship-shi-yo
너무 맵지 않는 것으로 주십시오

It's not hot.
um-shik-i ttŭ-kŏp-ji an-sŭm-ni-da
음식이 뜨겁지 않습니다

Is MSG used?
hwa-hak-jo-mi-ryo-rŭl nŏ-hŏss-sŭm-ni-kka?
화학조미료를 넣었습니까?

No MSG please.
hwa-hak-jo-mi-ryo-rŭl nŏ-ji ma-ship-shi-yo
화학조미료를 넣지 마십시오

The meal was delicious.
mat-it-ge jal mŏk-ŏss-sŭm-ni-da
맛있게 잘 먹었습니다

May I have the bill now, please?
kye-san-sŏ-rŭl ju-shi-gess-sŭm-ni-kka?
계산서를 주시겠습니까?

Please may I have a receipt?
yŏng-su-jŭng-ul ju-shi-gess-sŭm-ni-kka?
영수증을 주시겠습니까?

FOOD

Vegetarians

I am a vegetarian.
jŏ-nŭn ch'ae-shik-ju-ŭi-ja-im-ni-da   저는 채식주의자입니다

Do you have any vegetarian dishes?
ya-ch'ae yo-ri-ga iss-sŭm-ni-kka?   야채 요리가 있습니까?

I don't eat ...	... *mŏk-ji an-sŭm-ni-da*	... 먹지 않습니다
dairy products	*yu-je-p'um*	유제품
fish	*saeng-sŏn*	생선
pork	*dwae-ji-go-gi*	돼지고기
meat	*ko-gi*	고기

Breakfast

In country areas people eat big Korean-style meals. In the cities, due to the faster pace of life, people tend to have light, simple meals, and young people tend to have Western-style breakfasts. Hotel restaurants usually serve Western-style breakfasts which can be expensive, but you can buy less expensive food at supermarkets or from the food section of department stores.

FOOD

bacon	*be-i-k'ŏn*	베이컨
bread	*ppang*	빵
butter	*bŏ-t'ŏ*	버터
cornflakes	*k'on-p'ŭl-re-i-k'ŭ*	콘플레이크
eggs	*kye-ran*	계란
boiled eggs	*sal-mŭn kye-ran*	삶은 계란
fried eggs	*kye-ran-bu-ch'im*	계란부침
scrambled eggs	*bok-ŭn kye-ran*	볶은 계란

jam	*jaem*	잼
margarine	*ma-ga-rin*	마가린
milk	*u-yu*	우유
omelette	*o-mŭl-let*	오믈렛
toast	*t'o-sŭ-t'ŭ*	토스트
black coffee	*bŭl-laek k'ŏ-p'i*	블랙 커피
white coffee	*k'ŏ-p'i*	커피
tea	*hong-ch'a*	홍차

Lunch

Most dinner dishes are also available in restaurants for lunch. In the cities, most restaurants cater for workers wanting a quick meal. The following dishes are commonly eaten for lunch. Of course, there are also many fast food chain outlets.

Korean Dishes

된장 찌개   *doen-jang jji-gae*
    bean curd, meat and vegetables with
    soybean paste

만두국   *man-du-guk*
    dumplings with meat, vegetables and
    hot broth

갈비탕   *kal-bi-t'ang*
    rich beef broth with rice

군만두   *kun-man-du*
    fried dimsum

찐만두   *jjin-man-du*
    steamed dimsum

김밥   *kim-bap*
    Korean-style sushi

FOOD

비빔밥   *bi-bim-bap*
  rice, mixed with vegetables, meat and
  sauce

백반   *baek-ban*
  rice, soup, kimchi and side dishes

냉면   *naeng-myŏn*
  cold noodles in cold broth with
  vegetables

비빔 냉면   *bi-bim naeng-myŏn*
  cold noodles mixed with cold
  vegetables and sauce

막국수   *mak-guk-su*
  fresh noodles with vegetables, meat
  and chicken broth

콩국수   *k'ong-guk-su*
  fresh noodles in soybean broth

라면   *ra-myŏn*
  instant noodles

설렁탕   *sŏl-lŏng-t'ang*
  noodles with beef stock soup

매운탕   *mae-un-t'ang*
  fish soup with chilli

신선로   *shin-sŏn-ro*
  casserole of meat, fish, vegetables and
  bean curd

빈대떡   *bin-dae-ttŏk*
  Korean pancake

잡채   *jap-ch'ae*
  mixed noodles with vegetables and beef

FOOD

Chinese Dishes

야끼 만두	*ya-kki man-du*
Chinese fried dimsum	
볶음밥	*bok-ŭm-bap*
fried rice	
짜장면	*jja-jang-myŏn*
noodles, onions and pork with black sauce	
탕수육	*t'ang-su-yuk*
sweet and sour pork	

Dinner

The best way to try a wide range of Korean special dishes is to order the banquet meal, 한정식 (*han-jŏng-shik*); not cheap but delicious. There are also theatre restaurants which provide Korean meals along with traditional Korean dance and music. These are well worth experiencing.

Soup

콩나물국	bean sprout soup	*k'ong-na-mul-guk*
소고기국	beef soup	*so-go-gi-guk*
닭고기국	chicken soup	*dag-go-gi-guk*
만두국	dumpling soup	*man-du-guk*
미역국	seaweed soup	*mi-yŏk-guk*
된장국	soybean paste soup	*doen-jang-guk*

Beef

갈비찜	*kal-bi-jjim*
beef rib stew	
불고기	*bul-go-ki*
marinated beef fillet	

불갈비
  marinated beef ribs

bul-gal-bi

Pork

돼지불고기
  marinated pork fillet

dwae-ji-bul-go-gi

돼지갈비
  marinated pork ribs

dwae-ji-gal-bi

Seafood

생선전
  fried fish fillet

saeng-sŏn-jŏn

새우튀김
  fried prawns

sae-u-t'wi-gim

오징어볶음
  fried squid

o-jing-ŏ-bok-ŭm

생선찜
  steamed fish in sauce

saeng-sŏn-jjim

생선회
  raw fish

saeng-sŏn-hoe

Poultry

닭찜
  stewed chicken pieces with sauce

dag-jjim

삼계탕
  stewed chicken with ginseng and
  glutinous rice

sam-gye-t'ang

FOOD

Vegetables

Kimchi (pickled vegetable) is part of every Korean meal. It is Korea's popular authentic national dish. Kimchi is the generic term used for all spicy, pickled vegetables, each of which has a name. It is also the specific name for pickled cabbage.

콩나물   *k'ong-na-mul*
    boiled bean sprouts in sauce
가지무침   *ka-ji-mu-ch'im*
    boiled eggplant in sauce
시금치나물   *shi-gŭm-ch'i-na-mul*
    boiled spinach in sauce
호박전   *ho-bak-jŏn*
    fried baby pumpkin
두부튀김   *du-bu-t'wi-gim*
    fried bean curd
풋고추전   *p'ŭt-go-ch'u-jŏn*
    fried, stuffed young peppers
김치   *kim-ch'i*
    kimchi (pickled vegetable)
       배추김치   *bae-ch'u-kim-ch'i*
          Chinese cabbage
       오이김치   *o-i-kim-ch'i*
          stuffed cucumber

Dessert

Koreans do not customarily follow a meal with dessert. Fresh seasonal fruits are usually available, however.

Meat

beef	*so-go-gi*	소고기
chicken	*dag-go-gi*	닭고기
duck	*o-ri*	오리
goat	*yŏm-so*	염소
ham	*haem*	햄
lamb	*yang-go-gi*	양고기
liver	*kan*	간
meat	*ko-gi*	고기
pork	*dwae-ji-go-gi*	돼지고기
sausage	*so-shi-ji*	소시지

Seafood

abalone	*jŏn-bok*	전복
carp	*ing-ŏ*	잉어
clams	*dae-hap-jo-gae*	대합조개
cod	*dae-gu*	대구
crab	*ke*	게
eel	*baem-jang-ŏ*	뱀장어
fish	*mul-go-gi*	물고기
lobster	*ba-da-ga-jae*	바다가재
mussels	*hong-hap*	홍합
oysters	*kul*	굴
prawns	*k'ŭn-sae-u*	큰새우
sardines	*jŏng-ŏ-ri*	정어리
shark	*sang-ŏ*	상어
shellfish	*jo-gae*	조개
shrimp	*sae-u*	새우
squid	*o-jing-ŏ*	오징어
trout	*song-ŏ*	송어
tuna	*ch'am-ch'i*	참치

FOOD

Vegetables

beans	*k'ong*	콩
bean curd (tofu)	*du-bu*	두부
bean sprouts	*suk-ju*	숙주
cabbage	*yang-bae-ch'u*	양배추
carrot	*dang-gŭn*	당근
cauliflower	*kkot-yang-bae-ch'u*	꽃양배추
celery	*sel-lŏ-ri*	셀러리
corn	*ok-su-su*	옥수수
cucumber	*o-i*	오이
eggplant	*ka-ji*	가지
green pepper	*p'i-mang*	피망
lettuce	*sang-ch'u*	상추
mushrooms	*bŏ-sŏt*	버섯
olives	*ol-li-bŭ*	올리브
onion	*yang-p'a*	양파
peas	*wan-du-k'ong*	완두콩
potato	*kam-ja*	감자
pumpkin	*ho-bak*	호박
radish	*mu*	무
spinach	*shi-gŭm-ch'i*	시금치
spring onion	*dae-p'a*	대파
sweet potato	*ko-gu-ma*	고구마
tomato	*t'o-ma-t'o*	토마토
vegetables	*ch'ae-so*	채소

Fruit

apple	*sa-gwa*	사과
apricot	*sal-gu*	살구
avocado	*a-bo-k'a-do*	아보카도
banana	*ba-na-na*	바나나

blackberry	*kŏm-ŭn ttal-gi*	검은 딸기
cherries	*bŏ-jji*	버찌
dates	*dae-ch'u*	대추
figs	*mu-hwa-gwa*	무화과
fruit	*kwa-il*	과일
grapes	*p'o-do*	포도
grapefruit	*kŭ-re-i-p'ŭ-p'ŭ-ru-t'ŭ*	그레이프프루트
lemon	*re-mon*	레몬
mandarin	*kyul*	귤
melon	*ch'am-oe*	참외
orange	*o-ren-ji*	오렌지
peach	*bok-sung-a*	복숭아
pear	*bae*	배
persimmon	*kam*	감
pineapple	*p'a-in-ae-p'ŭl*	파인애플
plum	*ja-du*	자두
raisins	*kŏn-p'o-do*	건포도
strawberry	*ttal-gi*	딸기
watermelon	*su-bak*	수박

FOOD

Dairy Products

butter	*bŏ-t'ŏ*	버터
cheese	*ch'i-jŭ*	치즈
cream	*k'ŭ-rim*	크림
ice cream	*a-i-sŭ-k'ŭ-rim*	아이스크림
margarine	*ma-ga-rin*	마가린
milk	*u-yu*	우유
yoghurt	*yo-gu-rŭ-t'ŭ*	요구르트

Bread & Cereals

bread	*ppang*	빵
bread roll	*rol-ppang*	롤빵
rye bread	*ho-mil-ppang*	호밀빵
red bean paste bread	*ang-kko-ppang*	앙꼬빵
dry biscuits	*bi-sŭ-k'it*	비스킷
sweet biscuits	*dan bi-sŭ-k'it*	단 비스킷
barley	*bo-ri*	보리
corn	*ok-su-su*	옥수수
flour	*mil-ga-ru*	밀가루
oatmeal	*o-t'ŭ-mil*	오트밀
rice	*sal*	쌀
wheat	*mil*	밀

Condiments

black pepper	*hu-ch'u-ga-ru*	후추가루
chilli powder	*ko-ch'u-ga-ru*	고추가루
chilli sauce	*ko-ch'u-jang*	고추장
cinnamon	*kye-p'i*	계피
fish sauce	*saeng-sŏn-so-sŭ*	생선소스
garlic	*ma-nŭl*	마늘

FOOD

ginger	*saeng-gang*	생강
honey	*kkul*	꿀
mint	*bak-ha*	박하
mustard	*kyŏ-ja*	겨자
oil	*shik-yong-yu*	식용유
salt	*so-gŭm*	소금
soy sauce	*kan-jang*	간장
sugar	*sŏl-t'ang*	설탕
tomato sauce	*t'o-ma-t'o k'e-ch'ŏp*	토마토 케첩
vinegar	*shik-ch'o*	식초

Cooking Methods

barbecued	*ba-bi-k'yu*	바비큐
boiled	*sal-mŭn*	삶은
deep-fried	*t'wi-gin*	튀긴
fried	*bu-ch'in*	부친
grilled	*sŏk-soe-e ku-un*	석쇠에 구운
roasted	*o-bŭn-e ku-un*	오븐에 구운
steamed	*jjim*	찜

Drinks
Cold

barley tea	*bo-ri-ch'a*	보리차
soft drink	*sa-i-da*	사이다
cola	*k'ol-la*	콜라
grapefruit juice	*p'o-do ju-sŭ*	포도 주스
iced coffee	*naeng-k'ŏ-p'i*	냉커피
milk shake	*mil-k'ŭ sye-i-k'ŭ*	밀크 셰이크
mineral water	*t'an-san-su*	탄산수
orange juice	*o-ren-ji ju-sŭ*	오렌지 주스
peach juice	*bok-sung-a ju-sŭ*	복숭아 주스

FOOD

pineapple juice	*p'a-in-ae-p'ŭl ju-sŭ*	파인애플 주스
strawberry juice	*ttal-gi ju-sŭ*	딸기 주스
tomato juice	*t'o-ma-t'o ju-sŭ*	토마토 주스
drinking water	*saeng-su*	생수

Hot

black coffee	*bŭl-laek-k'ŏ-p'i*	블랙커피
white coffee	*k'ŏ-p'i*	커피
tea	*hong-ch'a*	홍차
arrowroot tea	*ch'ik-ch'a*	칡차
ginger tea	*saeng-gang-ch'a*	생강차
ginseng tea	*in-sam-ch'a*	인삼차
herb tea	*sang-hwa-ch'a*	쌍화차
Job's-tears tea	*yul-mu-ch'a*	율무차
sesame tea	*dŭl-kkae-ch'a*	들깨차
walnut tea	*ho-du-ch'a*	호두차

Alcoholic

beer	*maek-ju*	맥주
draught beer	*saeng-maek-ju*	생맥주
brandy	*bŭ-raen-di*	브랜디
cognac	*k'o-nyak*	코냑
gin	*jin*	진
Korean gin	*so-ju*	소주
port	*p'o-t'ŭ*	포트

FOOD

sherry	sye-ri	셰리
vermouth	bŏ-mon-t'ŭ	버몬트
vodka	bo-dŭ-k'a	보드카
whiskey	wi-sŭ-k'i	위스키
rice wine	jŏng-jong	정종
... wine	... p'o-do-ju	... 포도주
white	baek	백
red	jŏk	적
Korean	Han-guk-san	한국산
Australian	Ho-ju-san	호주산
French	P'ŭ-rang-sŭ-san	프랑스산
German	Do-gil-san	독일산

Some Useful Words & Phrases

What is the name of this restaurant?
i re-sŭ-t'o-rang i-rŭm-i mu-ŏt-im-ni-kka?
이 레스토랑 이름이 무엇입니까?

Is the water drinkable?
i mul ma-shil su id-gess-sŭm-ni-kka?
이 물 마실 수 있겠습니까?

This isn't my order.
i-gŏ-sun ju-mun an haess-sŭm-ni-da
이것은 주문 안 했습니다

Where are the toilets?
hwa-jang-shil-i ŏ-di-e iss-sŭm-ni-kka?
화장실이 어디에 있습니까?

ashtray	jae-ttŏl-i	재떨이
baby food	yu-a-shik	유아식
the bill	kye-san-sŏ	계산서

FOOD

bowl	*sa-bal*	사발
chopsticks	*jŏt-ga-rak*	젓가락
cup	*k'ŏp*	컵
fork	*p'o-k'ŭ*	포크
fresh	*shin-sŏn-han*	신선한
glass	*yu-ri-k'ŏp*	유리컵
hot (spicy)	*mae-un*	매운
knife	*na-i-p'ŭ*	나이프
menu	*me-nyu*	메뉴
plate	*jŏp-shi*	접시
salty	*jjan-mat*	짠맛
spoon	*sut-ga-rak*	숟가락
sweet	*dan-mat*	단맛
teaspoon	*t'i-sŭ-p'un*	티스푼
toothpick	*i-su-shi-gae*	이쑤시개

FOOD

Shopping

In Seoul, Itaewon is the shopping district that caters specifically for foreigners. You can buy just about anything you'd want and most shop assistants can speak English.

Korean culture has traditionally held many superstitions. One widely held superstition is that if the first customer of the day does not buy anything, then business will be bad all day. If you enter a shop early in the morning, make sure you intend to buy something.

How can I get to ...?	*...-e ŏ-ttŏ-ke kam-ni-kka?*	... 에 어떻게 갑니까?
the Dongdae-mun Market	*Dong-dae-mun-shi-jang*	동대문시장
Insadong	*In-sa-dong*	인사동
Itaewon	*I-t'ae-wŏn*	이태원
the Namdae-mun Market	*Nam-de-mun-shi-jang*	남대문시장

Is it far?
mŏl-li iss-sŭm-ni-kka? 멀리 있습니까?

Where can I buy ...?
... ŏ-di-e-sŏ sal su iss-sŭm-ni-kka? ... 어디에서 살 수 있습니까?

Where is the nearest ...?
i kŭn-ch'ŏ ... ŏ-di-e iss-sŭm-ni-kka? 이 근처 ... 어디에 있습니까?

antique shop *kol-dong-p'um-jŏm* 골동품점

129

art gallery	*hwa-rang*	화랑
bookshop	*sŏ-jŏm*	서점
camera shop	*k'a-me-ra-jŏm*	카메라점
clothing store	*ot-ga-ge*	옷가게
department store	*baek-hwa-jŏm*	백화점
dressmaker	*yang-jang-jŏm*	양장점
drycleaners	*se-t'ak-so*	세탁소
electronics shop	*jŏn-ja-je-p'um-jŏm*	전자제품점
ginseng shop	*in-sam-ga-ge*	인삼가게
jewellery shop	*bo-sŏk-sang*	보석상
market	*shi-jang*	시장
shoe shop	*shin-bal-ga-ge*	신발가게
shop	*ka-ge*	가게
souvenir shop	*ki-nyŏm-p'um-jŏm*	기념품점
sporting goods shop	*sŭ-p'o-ch'ŭ-yong-p'um-jŏm*	스포츠용품점
stationery shop	*mun-bang-gu-jŏm*	문방구점
supermarket	*syu-p'ŏ-ma-k'et*	슈퍼마켓
tailor	*yang-bok-jŏm*	양복점

Bargaining

Bargaining is traditional in Korea and is widely practised, except in bookshops and big department stores.

That's too expensive.
nŏ-mu bi-sam-ni-da   너무 비쌉니다

I'll buy it if you lower the price.
ka-gyŏk-ŭl kkak-a ju-shi-myŏn   가격을 깍아 주시면 사겠습니다
sa-gess-sŭm-ni-da

I don't have much money.
don-i jo-gŭm bak-e ŏb-sŭm-   돈이 조금 밖에 없습니다
ni-da

I'll give you ... won.
... wŏn-man ha-ship-shi-yo   ...원만 하십시오

I can't give you more
than ... won.
... wŏn i-sang mot dŭ-ri-gess-   ...원 이상 못 드리겠습니다
sŭm-ni-da

Making a Purchase

I would like to buy ...
... sa-ryŏ-go ham-ni-da   ... 사려고 합니다

How much is it?
ŏl-ma-im-ni-kka?   얼마입니까?
ŏl-ma-ye-yo? (inf)   얼마예요?

Do you have others?
da-rŭn kŏt iss-sŭm-ni-kka?   다른 것 있습니까?

I don't like it.
ma-ŭm-e an dŭm-ni-da   마음에 안 듭니다

I would like a better quality one.
p'um-jil-i dŏ jo-hŭn kŏ-sŭl ju-ship-shi-yo
품질이 더 좋은 것을 주십시오

Can I see it?
bwa-do doem-ni-kka?
봐도 됩니까?

I want something cheaper.
dŏ san kŏt-ŭ-ro ju-ship-shi-yo
더 싼 것으로 주십시오

I like this one.
i-kŏt jo-sŭm-ni-da
이것 좋습니다

I'm just looking.
ku-gyŏng-ha-go iss-sŭm-ni-da
구경하고 있습니다

What is it made of?
mu-sŭn jae-ryo-ro man-dŭl-ŏss-sŭm-ni-kka?
무슨 재료로 만들었습니까?

I want something like this.
i-rŏ-han kŏ-sŭl jo-ha-ham-ni-da
이러한 것을 좋아합니다

My size is ...
je sa-i-jŭ-nŭn ... im-ni-da
제 사이즈는 ... 입니다

Can I try it on?
ip-ŏ bwa-do doem-ni-kka?
입어 봐도 됩니까?

Where is the fitting room?
ŏ-di-sŏ ot kal-a ip-sŭm-ni-kka?
어디서 옷 갈아 입습니까?

It fits well.
jal mat-sŭm-ni-da
잘 맞습니다

It doesn't fit.
i-gŏn mat-ji an-sŭm-ni-da
이건 맞지 않습니다

Can it be altered?
ko-ch'il su iss-sŭm-ni-kka?
고칠 수 있습니까?

It is too ...	i-gŏ-sŭn nŏ-mu ...	이것은 너무 ...
big	k'ŭm-ni-da	큽니다
long	kil-ŏ-yo	길어요
loose	hŏl-lŏng-hae-yo	헐렁해요
short	jjal-ba-yo	짧아요
small	jak-a-yo	작아요
tight	kkok jjae-yo	꼭 째요

Can you write down the price?
ka-gyŏk-ŭl sŏ ju-shi-gess-sŭm-ni-kka?　　가격을 써 주시겠습니까?

Do you accept credit cards?
shin-yong-k'a-dŭ bat-sŭm-ni-kka?　　신용카드 받습니까?

Can I pay with travellers' cheques?
yŏ-haeng-ja su-p'yo-ro ji-bul-hae-do doem-ni-kka?　　여행자 수표로 지불해도 됩니까?

I would like a refund please.
ban-hwan-hae ju-ship-shi-yo　　반환해 주십시오

Can I exchange this?
i-gŏ-sŭl ba-kku-wŏ ju-shil su iss-sŭm-ni-kka?　　이것을 바꾸워 주실 수 있습니까?

Souvenirs

I'd like to buy some ...	... sa-ryŏ-go ham-ni-da	... 사려고 합니다
I'm interested in ...	... bo-go ship-sŭm-ni-da	... 보고 싶습니다
embroidered goods	su-ye-p'um	수예품
handcrafts	su-kong-ye-p'um	수공예품
jewellery	bo-sŏk	보석

Korean dolls	*Han-guk-in hyŏng*	한국인형
lacquerware	*ch'il-gi*	칠기
leatherwork	*p'i-hyŏk-je-p'um*	피혁제품
mother-of-pearl	*jin-ju*	진주
porcelain	*do-ja-gi*	도자기
pottery	*do-gi-ryu*	도기류
souvenirs	*ki-nyŏm-p'um*	기념품
traditional Korean dress	*Han-bok*	한복
traditional musical instruments	*Han-guk-ak-gi*	한국악기

Is it handmade?
su-gong-je-p'um-im-ni-kka? 수공제품입니까?

Clothing

swimsuit	*su-yŏng-bok*	수영복
dress	*dŭ-re-sŭ*	드레스
hat	*mo-ja*	모자
jacket	*jae-k'it*	재킷
jeans	*ch'ŏng-ba-ji*	청바지
jumper	*jam-ba*	잠바
overcoat	*oe-t'u*	외투
pullover	*p'ul-o-bŏ*	풀오버
pyjamas	*jam-ot*	잠옷
raincoat	*bi-ot*	비옷
shirt	*wa-i-syŏ-ch'ŭ*	와이셔츠
shoes	*ku-du*	구두
shorts	*ban-ba-ji*	반바지
skirt	*sŭ-k'ŏ-t'ŭ*	스커트

socks	*yang-mal*	양말
stockings	*sŭ-t'a-k'ing*	스타킹
trousers	*ba-ji*	바지
T-shirt	*t'i-syŏ-ch'ŭ*	티-셔츠
underwear	*nae-ŭi*	내의

Materials

cotton	*myŏn*	면
lace	*re-i-sŭ*	레이스
leather	*ka-juk*	가죽
polyester	*p'ol-li-e-sŭ-t'e-rŭ*	폴리에스테르
satin	*kong-dan*	공단
silk	*bi-dan*	비단
velvet	*bel-bet*	벨벳
wool	*yang-mo*	양모

Toiletries

baby powder	*be-i-bi p'a-u-dŏ*	베이비 파우더
baby's bottle	*jŏt-byŏng*	젖병
comb	*bit*	빗
(hair) conditioner	*rin-sŭ*	린스
condoms	*k'on-dom*	콘돔
deodorant	*bang-ch'wi-je*	방취제
face powder	*bun*	분
hairbrush	*he-ŏ-bŭ-rŏ-shi*	헤어브러시
lipstick	*rip-sŭ-t'ik*	립스틱
nail clippers	*son-t'op-kkak-gi*	손톱깎이
perfume	*hyang-su*	향수
razor	*myŏn-do-k'al*	면도칼
sanitary pads	*saeng-ri-dae*	생리대
shampoo	*syam-p'u*	샴푸

shaving cream	*myŏn-do k'ŭ-rim*	면도 크림
soap	*bi-nu*	비누
sunblock cream	*sŏn k'ŭ-rim*	썬 크림
talcum powder	*t'ael-k'ŏm p'a-u-dŏ*	탤컴 파우더
tampons	*t'am-p'on*	탐폰
tissues	*hyu-ji*	휴지
toilet paper	*hwa-jang-ji*	화장지
toothbrush	*ch'is-sol*	칫솔
toothpaste	*ch'i-yak*	치약
tweezers	*jok-jip-ge*	족집게

Stationery & Publications

book	*ch'aek*	책
guidebook in English	*Yŏng-mun kwan-gwang-an-nae-sŏ*	영문 관광안내서
novel in English	*Yŏng-ŏ so-sŏl*	영어 소설
Korean-English dictionary	*Han-Yŏng sa-jŏn*	한영 사전
envelopes	*bong-t'u*	봉투
magazine	*jap-ji*	잡지
map	*ji-do*	지도
map of the town	*shi-ga-ji ji-do*	시가지 지도
road map	*do-ro ji-do*	도로 지도
tourist map in English	*Yŏng-mun kwan-gwang-ji-do*	영문 관광지도
newspaper	*shin-mun*	신문
notebook	*no-t'ŭ*	노트

pen	*p'en*	펜
pencil	*yŏn-p'il*	연필
postcards	*yŏp-sŏ*	엽서
scissors	*ka-wi*	가위
writing paper	*p'yŏn-ji-ji*	편지지

Photography

I'd like a film for this camera.
i k'a-me-ra-e mat-nŭn p'il-rŭm-ŭl ju-ship-shi-yo   이 카메라에 맞는 필름을 주십시오

How much is it to develop?
hyŏn-sang ha-nŭn-de ŏl-ma-im-ni-kka?   현상 하는데 얼마입니까?

When will it be ready?
ŏn-je doem-ni-kka?   언제 됩니까?

Do you fix cameras?
k'a-me-ra ko-ch'yŏ ju-shil su iss-sŭm-ni-kka?   카메라 고쳐 주실 수 있습니까?

The camera is jammed.
p'il-lŭm-i dol-a-ga-ji an-sŭm-ni-da   필름이 돌아가지 않습니다

Do you sell video film?
bi-di-o t'e-i-p'ŭ pam-ni-kka?   비디오 테이프 팝니까?

I would like a roll of ...	... *han t'ong ju-ship-shi-yo*	... 한 통 주십시오
film	*p'il-lŭm*	필름
B&W film	*hŭk-baek p'il-lŭm*	흑백 필름
colour print film	*k'ŏl-lŏ p'il-lŭm*	컬러 필름
colour slide film	*k'ŏl-lŏ sŭl-la-i-dŭ*	컬러 슬라이드

battery	*bae-t'ŏ-ri*	배터리
camera	*k'a-me-ra*	카메라
flash	*p'ŭl-re-shi*	플래시
lens	*ren-jŭ*	렌즈
light metre	*no-ch'ul-kye*	노출계
video camera	*bi-di-o k'a-me-ra*	비디오 카메라

Smoking

Would you mind if I smoke?
    *dam-bae p'i-wŏ-do doem-
    ni-kka?*

담배 피워도 됩니까?

Would you like a cigarette?
    *dam-bae p'i-u-shi-gess-sŭm-
    ni-kka?*

담배 피우시겠습니까?

No thanks. I don't smoke.
    *a-ni-yo. dam-bae an p'i-um-
    ni-da*

아니오. 담배 안 피웁니다

Do you have a lighter?
    ra-i-t'ŏ iss-sŭm-ni-kka?

라이터 있습니까?

A packet of cigarettes, please.
    *dam-bae han kap ju-ship-
    shi-yo*

담배 한 갑 주십시오

cigarettes	*dam-bae*	담배
lighter	*ra-i-t'ŏ*	라이터
matches	*sŏng-nyang*	성냥
pipe	*dam-baet-dae*	담뱃대
tobacco	*t'o-ba-k'o*	토바코

Colours

beige	*be-i-ji*	베이지
black	*kŏm-jŏng*	검정
blue	*p'a-rang*	파랑
brown	*kal-saek*	갈색
dark	*ji-tŭn*	짙은
gold	*kŭm*	금
green	*ch'o-rok*	초록
grey	*hoe-saek*	회색
light	*yŏn-han*	연한
orange	*o-ren-ji*	오렌지
pink	*bun-hong*	분홍
purple	*bo-ra*	보라
red	*ppal-gang*	빨강
silver	*ŭn*	은
white	*ha-yan*	하얀
yellow	*no-rang*	노랑

Weights & Measures

gram	*kŭ-raem*	그램
kilogram	*k'il-lo-kŭ-raem*	킬로그램
millimetre	*mil-li-mi-t'ŏ*	밀리미터
centimetre	*sen-t'i-mi-t'ŏ*	센티미터
metre	*mi-t'ŏ*	미터
kilometre	*k'il-lo-mi-t'ŏ*	킬로미터
half a litre	*ban ri-t'ŏ*	반 리터
litre	*ri-t'ŏ*	리터

Sizes & Quantities

big	*k'ŭn*	큰
bigger	*dŏ k'ŭn*	더 큰

biggest	*je-il k'ŭn*	제일 큰
enough	*ch'ung-bun-han*	충분한
heavy	*mu-gŏ-un*	무거운
less	*bo-da jŏ-gŭn*	보다 적은
light	*ka-byŏ-un*	가벼운
a little bit	*jo-gŭm*	조금
long	*kin*	긴
more	*dŏ*	더
much/many	*man-hŭn*	많은
small	*ja-gŭn*	작은
smaller	*dŏ ja-gŭn*	더 작은
smallest	*je-il ja-gŭn*	제일 작은
too much	*nŏ-mu man-hŭn*	너무 많은

Some Useful Words

bag	*ka-bang*	가방
button	*dan-ch'u*	단추
discount	*hal-in*	할인
needle (sewing)	*ba-nŭl*	바늘
thread	*shil*	실
receipt	*yŏng-su-jŭng*	영수증
watch	*shi-gye*	시계
umbrella	*u-san*	우산

Health

As a result of its industrialisation and high population density, Korea has significant air and water pollution, especially in big cities. People with respiratory or cardiac problems, or with sensitive stomachs, should ensure that they have adequate preventative medications. Avoid ice and drinking tap water, and check whether water from other sources is suitable for drinking. There are five kinds of health services available – Western-style general hospitals, oriental medicine clinics, health clinics, private doctor's clinics and chemists. Western-style general hospitals provide services similar to those in Western countries and have some English-speaking doctors. Oriental medicine clinics use traditional therapies which include herbal medicines, acupuncture and acupressure. These treatments have been used for over a thousand years. Government-run health clinics are located in all parts of Korea. There are numerous private doctors' clinics and you usually do not need an appointment, even for specialists. You are able to buy medication from any chemist without a doctor's prescription.

If you are currently taking medication, or need to take medication intermittently, make sure you take an adequate supply for your stay in Korea. Medication produced abroad is very expensive in Korea.

I am sick.
mom-i a-p'ŭm-ni-da   몸이 아픕니다

My ... is sick.	*je ... a-p'ŭm-ni-da*	제 ... 아픕니다
husband	*nam-p'yŏn*	남편
wife	*a-nae*	아내
child	*a-i*	아이
friend	*ch'in-gu*	친구

Call an ambulance.
ku-gŭp-ch'a bul-lŏ-ju-ship-shi-yo   구급차 불러 주십시오

I need a doctor.
ŭi-sa-ga p'il-yo-ham-ni-da   의사가 필요합니다

I'd like a female doctor.
yŏ-ja-ŭi-sa-rŭl bu-t'ak-ham-ni-da   여자의사를 부탁합니다

Where can I find a good doctor?
jo-hŭn ŭi-sa-ga ŏ-di-e iss-sŭm-ni-kka?   좋은 의사가 어디에 있습니까?

Could you please call a doctor?
ŭi-sa-rŭl bul-lŏ ju-shi-gess-sŭm-ni-kka?   의사를 불러 주시겠습니까?

When can the doctor come?
myŏt shi-e ol su iss-sŭm-ni-kka?   몇 시에 올 수 있습니까?

Where is ...?	*... ŏ-di-e iss-sŭm-ni-kka?*	... 어디에 있습니까?
an acupuncturist	*ch'im-sul-ŭi-wŏn*	침술의원
the chemist	*yak-guk*	약국

a dentist	*ch'i-gwa-ŭi*	치과의
a doctor	*ŭi-sa*	의사
the hospital	*byŏng-wŏn*	병원

Symptoms

I have a headache.
mŏ-ri-ka a-p'ŭm-ni-da   머리가 아픕니다

I feel dizzy.
ŏ-ji-rŏp-sŭm-ni-da   어지럽습니다

I feel weak.
him-i ŏbs-sŭm-ni-da   힘이 없습니다

I feel very thirsty.
mae-u mo-gi ma-rŭm-ni-da   매우 목이 마릅니다

I have an itch.
ka-ryŏp-sŭm-ni-da   가렵습니다

I've been bitten by something.
mu-ŏt-e mul-ryŏss-sŭm-ni-da   무엇에 물렸습니다

I'm having trouble breathing.
sum-swi-gi-ga him-dŭm-ni-da   숨쉬기가 힘듭니다

I have no appetite.
im-ma-shi ŏbs-sŭm-ni-da   입맛이 없습니다

I feel nauseated.
ku-yŏk-jil-i nam-ni-da   구역질이 납니다

I've been vomiting.
t'o-haess-sŭm-ni-da   토했습니다

I've had diarrhoea.
sŏl-sa-ga nam-ni-da   설사가 납니다

I can't sleep.
jam-i an op-ni-da   잠이 안 옵니다

I have difficulty passing urine.
so-byŏn bo-gi-ga him-dŭm-ni-da   소변 보기가 힘듭니다

It hurts here.
yŏ-gi-ga a-p'ŭm-ni-da   여기가 아픕니다

Allergies

I have a skin allergy.
p'i-bu al-le-rŭ-gi iss-sŭm-ni-da   피부 알레르기 있습니다

I'm allergic to ...	... al-le-rŭ-gi iss-sŭm-ni-da	... 알레르기 있습니다
antibiotics	hang-saeng-je	항생제
aspirin	a-sŭ-p'i-rin	아스피린
codeine	k'o-de-in	코데인
dairy products	u-yu je-p'um	우유제품
MSG	hwa-hak-jo-mi-ryo	화학조미료
penicillin	p'e-ni-shil-lin	페니실린

Ailments

I have ...	... iss-sŭm-ni-da	... 있습니다
You have ...	... im-ni-da	... 입니다
I think it's ...	... in kŏs kat-sŭm-ni-da	... 인 것 같습니다
anaemia	bin-hyŏl	빈혈
appendicitis	maeng-jang-yŏm	맹장염
asthma	ch'ŏn-shik	천식
a bacterial infection	bak-t'e-ri-a yŏm-jŭng	박테리아 염증
a cold	kam-gi	감기

constipation	*byŏn-bi*	변비
a cough	*ki-ch'im*	기침
cystitis	*bang-gwang-yŏm*	방광염
dehydration	*t'al-su*	탈수
diarrhoea	*sŏl-sa*	설사
an ectopic pregnancy	*ja-gung-oe im-shin*	자궁외 임신
eczema	*sŭp-jin*	습진
epilepsy	*kan-jil-byŏng*	간질병
a fever	*yŏl*	열
food poisoning	*shik-jung-dok*	식중독
frostbite	*dong-sang*	동상
gastroenteritis	*wi-san-gwa-da-jŭng*	위산과다증
glandular fever	*sŏn-yŏl*	선열
haemorrhoids	*ch'i-jil*	치질
a heart condition	*shim-jang-byŏng*	심장병
hepatitis	*kan-yŏm*	간염
hypertension	*ko-hyŏl-ap*	고혈압
indigestion	*so-hwa-bul-ryang*	소화불량
an infection	*jŏn-yŏm-byŏng*	전염병
an inflammation	*yŏm-jŭng*	염증
influenza	*dok-gam*	독감
lice	*i*	이
malaria	*mal-la-ri-a*	말라리아
measles	*hong-yŏk*	홍역
a migraine	*shim-han du-t'ong*	심한 두통
morning sickness	*im-shin-gu-t'o-jŭng*	임신구토증
mumps	*yu-haeng-sŏng i-ha-sŏn-yŏm*	유행성 이하선염
pneumonia	*p'ye-ryŏm*	폐렴
sunburn	*haet-byŏt-e t'am*	햇볕에 탐

sunstroke	*il-sa-byŏng*	일사병
tonsillitis	*p'yŏn-do-sŏn-yŏm*	편도선염
typhoid	*jang-jil-bu-sa*	장질부사
a urinary infection	*yo-do-yŏm*	요도염
a venereal disease	*sŏng-byŏng*	성병
a viral infection	*ba-i-rŏ-sŭ yŏm-jŭng*	바이러스 염증
worms	*ki-saeng-ch'ung*	기생충

You May Hear

You are pregnant.
im-shin ha-syŏss-sŭm-ni-da   임신 하셨습니다

It's broken.
bu-rŏ-jyŏss-sŭm-ni-da   부러졌습니다

It's dislocated.
t'al-ku doe-ŏss-sŭm-ni-da   탈구 되었습니다

It's sprained.
ppi-ŏss-sŭm-ni-da   삐었습니다

I want to ...	... *ha-syŏ-ya doe-gess-sŭm-ni-da*	... 하셔야 되겠습니다
admit you to hospital	*ip-wŏn*	입원
do a blood test	*hyŏl-aek-gŏm-sa*	혈액검사
do a urine test	*so-byŏn-gŏm-sa*	소변검사
take an ECG	*shim-jŏn-do*	심전도
take an x-ray	*ek-sŭ-sŏn ch'wal-yŏng*	엑스선 촬영

HEALTH

Parts of the Body

My ... hurts.	... *a-p'ŭm-ni-da*	... 아픕니다
I can't move my ...	... *um-ji-gil su ŏbs-sŭm-ni-da*	... 움직일 수 없습니다
My ... is swollen.	... *bu-ŏss-sŭm-ni-da*	... 부었습니다
arm	*p'al*	팔
back	*dŭng*	등
breast	*yu-bang*	유방
chest	*ka-sŭm*	가슴
ear	*kwi*	귀
eye	*nun*	눈
finger	*son-ga-rak*	손가락
gland	*sŏn*	선
foot	*bal*	발
hand	*son*	손
head	*mŏ-ri*	머리
hip	*ŏng-dŏng-i*	엉덩이
joint	*kwan-jŏl*	관절
knee	*mu-rŭp*	무릎
leg	*da-ri*	다리
mouth	*ip*	입
muscle	*kŭn-yuk*	근육
neck	*mok*	목
nose	*k'o*	코
shoulder	*ŏ-kkae*	어깨
stomach	*wi*	위
throat	*mok-gu-mŏng*	목구멍
tongue	*hyŏ*	혀
tonsils	*p'yŏn-do-sŏn*	편도선
toe	*bal-ga-rak*	발가락

HEALTH

At the Chemist

Chemists in Korea are quite different from most Western chemists. You are able to buy medication without a doctor's prescription. Korean people usually go to the chemist and explain their symptoms to the pharmacist who is then able to recommend and sell the necessary medication.

Where's the nearest chemist?
i kŭn-ch'ŏ-e yak-guk-i ŏ-di iss-sŭm-ni-kka?
이 근처에 약국이 어디 있습니까?

What time does the chemist open?
yak-guk-i myŏt shi-e yŏl-lim-ni-kka?
약국이 몇 시에 열립니까?

I need something for ...
... jom ju-ship-shi-yo
... 좀 주십시오

Do I need a prescription for ...?
... sa-ryŏ-myŏn ch'ŏ-bang-i iss-ŏ-ya ham-ni-kka?
...사려면 처방이 있어야 합니까?

How many times a day?
ha-ru-e myŏt bŏn mŏk-sŭm-ni-kka?
하루에 몇 번 먹습니까?

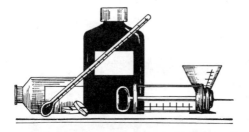

... times a day	*ha-ru-e ... bŏn*	하루에 ... 번
before each meal	*shik-jŏn*	식전
after each meal	*shik-hu*	식후
in the mornings	*a-ch'im*	아침
at night	*jŏ-nyŏ-ge*	저녁에

I would like to buy some ...	*... ju-ship-shi-yo*	... 주십시오
antibiotics	*hang-saeng-je*	항생제
antiseptic	*so-dok-yak*	소독약
aspirin	*a-sŭ-p'i-rin*	아스피린
Band-aids	*ban-ch'an-go*	반찬고
condoms	*k'on-dom*	콘돔
contraceptive pills	*p'i-im-yak*	피임약
cough medicine	*ki-ch'im-yak*	기침약
ear drops	*kwi-yak*	귀약
eye drops	*an-yak*	안약
laxatives	*byŏn-bi-yak*	변비약
pain-killers	*jin-t'ong-je*	진통제
sanitary pads	*saeng-ri-dae*	생리대
sleeping tablets	*su-myŏn-je*	수면제
tampons	*t'am-p'on*	탐폰
vitamins	*bi-t'a-min*	비타민

I would like to buy a thermo-meter.

ch'e-on-gi ju-ship-shi-yo   체온계 주십시오

HEALTH

At the Dentist

Is there a good dentist here?
  i kŭn-ch'ŏ-e jo-hŭn ch'i-gwa-
  ŭi-sa-ga iss-sŭm-ni-kka?

이 근처에 좋은 치과의사가
있습니까?

I have a toothache.
  i-ga a-p'ŭm-ni-da

이가 아픕니다

I don't want it extracted.
  i ppop-nŭn kŏt wŏn-ha-ji
  an-sŭm-ni-da

이 뽑는 것 원하지 않습니다

Please give me an anaesthetic.
  ma-ch'wi-je-rŭl ju-ship-shi-yo

마취제를 주십시오

Some Useful Phrases

I'm pregnant.
  im-shin hae-sŭm-ni-da

임신 했습니다

I'm on the (contraceptive) pill.
  p'i-im-ya-gŭl sa-yong-ha-go
  iss-sŭm-ni-da

피임약을 사용하고 있습니다

I haven't had my period for ...
months.
  ... dal saeng-ri-ga ŏbs-ŏss-
  sŭm-ni-da

... 달 생리가 없었습니다

Can you fix my glasses?
  an-gyŏng jom ko-ch'yŏ ju-
  shi-gess-sŭm-ni-kka?

안경 좀 고쳐 주시겠습니까?

I need a new pair of glasses.
  sae an-gyŏng-i p'il-yo-ham-
  ni-da

새 안경이 필요합니다

How much is the treatment?
  ch'i-ryo-bi-yong-i ŏl-ma-im-
  ni-kka?

치료비용이 얼마입니까?

May I have a receipt in English, please?

yŏng-ŏ-ro yŏng-su-jŭng jom ju-shi-gess-sŭm-ni-kka?

영어로 영수증 좀 주시겠습니까?

Thank you for helping me.

ch'i-ryo-hae ju-syŏ-sŏ kam-sa-ham-ni-da

치료해 주셔서 감사합니다

I have had a tetanus vaccination lately.

ch'oe-gŭn-e p'a-sang-p'ung ye-bang-ju-sa-rŭl ma-ja-sŭm-ni-da

최근에 파상풍 예방주사를 맞았습니다

When can I travel again?

ŏn-je yŏ-haeng da-shi hal su iss-sŭm-ni-kka?

언제 여행 다시 할 수 있습니까?

When can I leave hospital?

ŏn-je t'oe-wŏn hal su iss-sŭm-ni-kka?

언제 퇴원 할 수 있습니까?

Some Useful Words

accident	*sa-ko*	사고
acupuncture	*ch'im*	침
addiction	*jung-dok*	중독
anti-diarrhoeal drug	*ji-sa-je*	지사제
bandage	*bung-dae*	붕대
bite (dog)	*mul-lim (kae)*	물림(개)
bite (insect)	*mul-lim (bŏl-le)*	물림(벌레)
bleeding	*ch'ul-hyŏl*	출혈
blood group	*p'i-hyŏng*	피형
blood pressure	*hyŏl-ap*	혈압

blood test	*p'i gŏm-sa*	피검사
contagious	*jŏn-yŏm-sŏng-ŭi*	전염성의
delirious	*hŏt-so-ri-rŭl ha-nŭn*	헛소리를 하는
diabetes	*dang-nyo-byŏng*	당뇨병
dressing	*dŭ-re-shing*	드레싱
first aid kit	*ku-gŭp-ch'i-ryo-sang-ja*	구급치료상자
gauze	*kŏ-jŭ*	거즈
injection	*ju-sa*	주사
injury	*sang-hae*	상해
medicine	*yak*	약
nausea	*me-sŭ-kkŏ-um*	메스꺼움
ointment	*yŏn-ko*	연고
oxygen	*san-so*	산소
medical specialist	*jŏn-mun-ŭi-sa*	전문 의사
urine	*so-byŏn*	소변
wound	*sang-ch'ŏ*	상처

HEALTH

Time, Dates & Festivals

Telling the Time

Telling the time in Korean is similar to that in English. You state the hour first, then the minutes (see Numbers & Amounts, page 161) and add the suffix meaning 'o'clock'. The pure Korean version of numbers is used with hours – 시 (*shi*). The Chinese-derived version is used with minutes – 분 (*bun*).

What time is it?
   myŏt shi im-ni-kka?   몇 시 입니까?

It is ...	... *im-ni-da*	...입니다
9 am	*o-jŏn a-hop-shi*	오전 아홉시
7 pm	*o-hu il-gop-shi*	오후 일곱시
1.05	*han-shi o-bun*	한시 오분
3.15	*se-shi ship-o-bun*	세시 십오분
6.30	*yŏ-sŏs-shi ban*	여섯시 반
8.40	*yŏ-dŏl-shi sa-ship-bun*	여덟시 사십분
11.55	*yŏl-han-shi o-ship-o-bun*	열한시 오십오분
12.00	*yŏl-du-shi*	열두시

Some Useful Words & Phrases

What time does the bus leave?
   bŏ-sŭ-ga myŏt shi-e ch'ul-bal-ham-ni-kka?

버스가 몇 시에
출발합니까?

153

TIMES, DATES & FESTIVALS

The bus leaves at 10.30 pm.
jŏ-nyŏk yŏl-shi ban-e ch'ul-bal-
ham-ni-da

저녁 열시 반에
출발합니다

What time does it open?
myŏt shi-e yŏl-lim-ni-kka?

몇 시에 열립니까?

It opens at 9 am.
o-jŏn a-hop-shi-e yŏl-lim-ni-da

오전 아홉시에 열립니다

What time does it close?
myŏt shi-e das-sŭm-ni-kka?

몇 시에 닫습니까?

It closes at 4 pm.
o-hu ne-shi-e das-sŭm-ni-da

오후 네시에 닫습니다

in the morning	*a-ch'im-e*	아침에
in the afternoon	*o-hu-e*	오후에
in the evening	*jŏ-nyŏk-e*	저녁에
o'clock	*shi*	시
am	*o-jŏn*	오전
pm	*o-hu*	오후
minutes	*bun*	분
hours	*shi-gan*	시간

Days of the Week

Monday	*wŏl-yo-il*	월요일
Tuesday	*hwa-yo-il*	화요일
Wednesday	*su-yo-il*	수요일
Thursday	*mok-yo-il*	목요일
Friday	*kŭm-yo-il*	금요일
Saturday	*t'o-yo-il*	토요일
Sunday	*il-yo-il*	일요일

Months

January	*il-wŏl*	일월
February	*i-wŏl*	이월
March	*sam-wŏl*	삼월
April	*sa-wŏl*	사월
May	*o-wŏl*	오월
June	*yu-wŏl*	유월
July	*ch'il-wŏl*	칠월
August	*p'al-wŏl*	팔월
September	*ku-wŏl*	구월
October	*shi-wŏl*	시월
November	*ship-il-wŏl*	십일월
December	*ship-i-wŏl*	십이월

Seasons

spring	*bom*	봄
summer	*yŏ-rŭm*	여름
autumn	*ka-ŭl*	가을
winter	*kyŏ-ul*	겨울

Dates

Korean dates are usually written in the order of year, month and day. So, 25 December 1995 is written as 1995 년 (*nyŏn*) 12 월 (*wŏl*) 25 일 (*il*).

What date is it today?
o-nŭl myŏ-ch'il im-ni-kka?   오늘 며칠 입니까?

It is ...	... *im-ni-da*	... 입니다
1 January	*il-wŏl il-il*	일월 일일
15 June	*yu-wŏl ship-o-il*	유월 십오일

Present

today	o-nŭl	오늘
this morning	o-nŭl a-ch'im	오늘 아침
this afternoon	o-nŭl o-hu	오늘 오후
tonight	o-nŭl jŏ-nyŏk	오늘 저녁
this week	i-bŏn ju	이번 주
this month	i-bŏn dal	이번 달
this year	ol-hae	올해
immediately	kot	곧
now	ji-gŭm	지금

Past

yesterday ...	ŏ-je ...	어제...
morning	a-ch'im	아침
afternoon	o-hu	오후
evening	jŏ-nyŏk	저녁
day before yester-day	kŭ-jŏ-kke	그저께
two days ago	i-t'ŭl-jŏn	이틀전
a while ago	ŏl-ma jŏn-e	얼마 전에
last night	ŏ-jet-bam	어젯밤
last week	ji-nan ju	지난 주
last month	ji-nan dal	지난 달
last year	jak-nyŏn	작년

Future

tomorrow ...	nae-il ...	내일...
morning	a-ch'im	아침
afternoon	o-hu	오후
evening	jŏ-nyŏk	저녁

| day after tomorrow | *mo-re* | 모레 |
| two days after tomorrow | *kŭl-p'i* | 글피 |

next ...	*da-ŭm ...*	다음...
week	*ju*	주
month	*dal*	달
year	*hae*	해

During the Day

sunrise	*hae-do-ti*	해돋이
dawn	*a-ch'im il-jjik*	아침 일찍
morning	*a-ch'im*	아침
noon (midday)	*jŏng-o*	정오
afternoon	*o-hu*	오후
sunset	*hae-nŏm-i*	해넘이
evening	*jŏ-nyŏk*	저녁
midnight	*ja-jŏng*	자정

Some Useful Words & Phrases

century	*se-gi*	세기
day	*nal*	날
fortnight	*du ju-il*	두 주일
month	*dal*	달
night	*bam*	밤
week	*ju-il*	주일
year	*nyŏn*	년
... years ago	*... nyŏn jŏn-e*	... 년 전에
during the day	*nat-e*	낮에
during the week	*ju-jung-e*	주중에
weekday	*p'yŏng-il*	평일
weekend	*ju-mal*	주말

Religious & National Holidays

1 & 2 Jan	New Year's Day	*shin-jŏng*	신정/설날
1 Jan *	Lunar New Year's Day	*ku-jŏng*	구정/설날
1 Mar	Independence Day	*sam-il-jŏl*	삼일절
5 Apr	Arbor Day	*shik-mo-gil*	식목일
8 Apr *	Buddha's Birthday	*sŏk-ka t'an-shin-il*	석가 탄신일
5 May	Children's Day	*ŏ-rin-i nal*	어린이 날
6 Jun	Memorial Day	*hyŏn-ch'ung-il*	현충일
17 Jul	Constitution Day	*je-hŏn-jŏl*	제헌절
15 Aug	Liberation Day	*kwang-bok-jŏl*	광복절
15 Aug *	Korean Thanks-giving Day	*ch'u-sŏk*	추석
1 Oct	Armed Forces Day	*kuk-kun-ŭi nal*	국군의 날
3 Oct	National Foundation Day	*kae-ch'ŏn-jŏl*	개천절
9 Oct	Hangul Day	*han-kŭl-nal*	한글날
25 Dec	Christmas Day	*sŏng-t'an-jŏl*	성탄절

* by Lunar calendar

Some Important Holidays

New Year's Day (1-2 Jan)

The first two days of the New Year are celebrated. Family members get up early and put on their best clothes. The younger members bow to their parents and grandparents as a reaffirmation of family ties.

Korean New Year's Day (1 Jan by Lunar Calendar)

It is celebrated in a similar way to 1 January, but on a grander scale. Families carry out ceremonies to commemorate their ancestors. Various traditional games are played. There is much singing and traditional food is eaten.

Korean Thanksgiving Day (15 Aug by Lunar Calendar – full moon)

Korea's most important national holiday. People visit family tombs and present food offerings to their ancestors.

Some Useful Words & Phrases

after	*hu-e*	후에
always	*ŏn-je-na*	언제나
before	*jŏn-e*	전에
early	*il-jjik*	일찍
everyday	*mae-il*	매일
forever	*yŏng-wŏn-hi*	영원히
holiday	*hyu-il*	휴일
holidays	*hyu-ga*	휴가
late	*nŭt-ge*	늦게
later	*na-jung-e*	나중에
long ago	*o-rae jŏn-e*	오래 전에
never	*jŏn-hyŏ*	전혀

not any more	*dŏ i-sang*	더 이상
not yet	*a-jik*	아직
public holiday	*kong-hyu-il*	공휴일
recently	*ch'oe-gŭn-e*	최근에
school holidays	*bang-hak*	방학
sometimes	*ka-kkŭm*	가끔
soon	*kot*	곧

Numbers & Amounts

The first nine numbers need to be learnt, along with the tens from 10 to 90 and the words for 100, 1000, 10,000, etc. After that, combine each of the first nine numbers with the 10s, 100s, 1000s and so on, to make larger numbers. To make 15, take the word for 10, 십 (*ship*), and combine it with five, 오 (*o*), to derive 15, 십오 (*ship-o*).

Although Arabic numerals are used, there are two systems of pronouncing numbers in Korean – pure Korean and Chinese-derived. Korean numbers (which only go up to 99) are generally used when referring to things and hours. The Chinese-derived numbers are used to count money, days, mileage and minutes.

Cardinal Numbers

	Chinese-derived		Korean	
0	영	*yŏng*	공	*kong*
1	일	*il*	하나	*ha-na*
2	이	*i*	둘	*dul*
3	삼	*sam*	셋	*set*
4	사	*sa*	넷	*net*
5	오	*o*	다섯	*da-sŏt*
6	육	*yuk*	여섯	*yŏ-sŏt*
7	칠	*ch'il*	일곱	*il-gop*
8	팔	*p'al*	여덟	*yŏ-dŏl*
9	구	*ku*	아홉	*a-hop*
10	십	*ship*	열	*yŏl*
11	십일	*ship-il*	열하나	*yŏl-ha-na*

12	십이	*ship-i*	열둘	*yŏl-dul*
13	십삼	*ship-sam*	열셋	*yŏl-set*
14	십사	*ship-sa*	열넷	*yŏl-net*
15	십오	*ship-o*	열다섯	*yŏl-da-sŏt*
16	십육	*ship-yuk*	열여섯	*yŏl-yŏ-sŏt*
17	십칠	*ship-ch'il*	열일곱	*yŏl-il-gop*
18	십팔	*ship-p'al*	열여덟	*yŏl-yŏ-dŏl*
19	십구	*ship-gu*	열아홉	*yŏl-a-hop*
20	이십	*i-shpi*	스물	*sŭ-mul*
30	삼십	*sam-ship*	서른	*sŏ-rŭn*
40	사십	*sa-ship*	마흔	*ma-hŭn*
50	오십	*o-ship*	쉰	*swin*
60	육십	*yuk-ship*	예순	*ye-sun*
70	칠십	*ch'il-ship*	일흔	*il-hŭn*
80	팔십	*p'al-ship*	여든	*yŏ-dŭn*
90	구십	*ku-ship*	아흔	*a-hŭn*
99	구십구	*ku-ship-gu*	아흔아홉	*a-hŭn-a-hop*
100	백	*baek*		
101	백일	*bae-gil*		
200	이백	*i-baek*		
300	삼백	*sam-baek*		
400	사백	*sa-baek*		
500	오백	*o-baek*		
600	육백	*yuk-baek*		
700	칠백	*ch'il-baek*		
800	팔백	*p'al-baek*		
900	구백	*ku-baek*		
1000	천	*ch'ŏn*		
10,000	만	*man*		
100 million	억	*ŏk*		
one billion	조	*jo*		

NUMBERS

Counting Days

Chinese-derived			Korean	
one day	일일	*il-il*	하루	*ha-ru*
two days	이일	*i-il*	이틀	*i-t'ŭl*
three days	삼일	*sam-il*	사흘	*sa-hŭl*
four days	사일	*sa-il*	나흘	*na-hŭl*
five days	오일	*o-il*	닷새	*dat-se*
six days	육일	*yu-gil*	엿새	*yŏt-sae*
seven days	칠일	*ch'il-il*	이레	*i-rae*
eight days	팔일	*p'al-il*	여드레	*yŏ-dŭ-re*
nine days	구일	*ku-il*	아흐레	*a-hŭ-re*
ten days	십일	*ship-il*	열흘	*yŏl-hŭl*

NUMBERS

Ordinal Numbers

1st	*ch'ŏt-jjae bŏn*	첫째 번
2nd	*dul-jjae bŏn*	둘째 번
3rd	*set-jjae bŏn*	셋째 번
4th	*net-jjae bŏn*	넷째 번
5th	*da-sŏt-jjae bŏn*	다섯째 번

Fractions

1/4	*sa-bun-ji il*	사분지 일
1/3	*sam-bun-ji il*	삼분지 일
1/2	*i-bun-ji il*	이분지 일
3/4	*sa-bun-ji sam*	사분지 삼

Some Useful Words

calculate	*kye-san-ha-da*	계산하다
calculator	*kye-san-gi*	계산기

add	*dŏ-ha-da*	더하다
substract	*ppae-da*	빼다
multiply	*kop-ha-da*	곱하다
divide	*na-nu-da*	나누다
a little (amount)	*yang-i jŏ-gŭn*	양이 적은
count	*su-rŭl se-da*	수를 세다
double	*du bae*	두 배
a dozen	*da-sŭ/t'a*	다스/타
Enough!	*ch'ung-bun-hae-yo!*	충분해요!
few	*su-ga jŏ-gŭn*	수가 적은
less	*bo-da jŏ-gŭn*	보다 적은
a lot	*man-hŭn*	많은
many	*su-ga man-hŭn*	수가 많은
more	*dŏ*	더
a pair	*sang*	쌍
percent	*p'ŏ-sen-t'ŭ*	퍼센트
too much	*yang-i man-hŭn*	양이 많은
twice	*du-bŏn*	두번
once	*han-bŏn*	한번

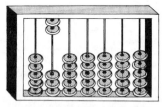

Vocabulary

A

aboard	*kuk-oe-ro*	국외로
about (approxi-mately)	*dae-ryak*	대략
above	*wi-e*	위에
accept	*bat-da*	받다
accident	*sa-go*	사고
accommodation	*suk-bak-shi-sŏl*	숙박시설
across	*mat-ŭn-p'yŏn-e*	맞은편에
adaptor	*ŏ-daep-t'ŏ*	어댑터
addiction	*jung-dok*	중독
address	*ju-so*	주소
administration	*kwan-ri*	관리
admission	*ip-jang*	입장
advantage	*jang-jŏm*	장점
adventure	*mo-hŏm*	모험
advice	*ch'ung-go*	충고
advise	*jung-go-ha-da*	충고하다
aeroplane	*bi-haeng-gi*	비행기
afraid	*kŏk-jŏng-ha-nŭn*	걱정하는
after	*hu-e*	후에
afternoon	*o-hu*	오후
again	*da-shi*	다시
against	*ban-dae-ha-yŏ*	반대하여
age	*na-i*	나이
agree	*dong-ŭi-ha-da*	동의하다
Do you agree?	*dong-ŭi-ha-shim-ni-kka?*	동의 하십니까?

agriculture	*nong-ŏp*	농업
ahead	*ap-jjok-e*	앞쪽에
aid	*dop-da*	돕다
air-conditioned	*e-ŏ-k'ŏn*	에어컨
airmail	*hang-kong-u-p'yŏn*	항공우편
airport	*bi-haeng-jang*	비행장
alarm clock	*ja-myŏng-jong*	자명종
all	*mo-dŭn*	모든
allow	*hŏ-rak-ha-da*	허락하다
almost	*kŏ-ŭi*	거의
alone	*hon-ja*	혼자
also	*tto-han*	또한
always	*hang-sang*	항상
amazing	*nol-lal-man-han*	놀랄만한
ambassador	*dae-sa*	대사
among	*jung-e*	중에
ancient	*o-rae-doen*	오래된
and	*kŭ-ri-go*	그리고
angry	*sŏng-nan*	성난
animal	*dong-mul*	동물
answer (v)	*dae-dap-ha-da*	대답하다
antique	*kol-dong-p'um*	골동품
any	*ŏ-ttŏ-han*	어떠한
anything	*mu-ŏ-shi-dŭn-ji*	무엇이든지
appointment	*ye-yak*	예약
approximately	*dae-ryak*	대략
argue	*non-jaeng-ha-da*	논쟁하다
argument	*non-jaeng*	논쟁
arrive	*do-ch'ak-ha-da*	도착하다
art	*ye-sul*	예술
ashtray	*kae-ttŏ-ri*	재떨이

ask	*mut-da*	묻다
at	*-e*	-에
automatic	*ja-dong*	자동

B

baby	*a-ki*	아기
babysitter	*a-ki bo-nŭn sa-ram*	아기 보는 사람
backpack	*bae-nang*	배낭
bad	*na-ppŭn*	나쁜
bag	*ka-bang*	가방
baggage	*su-hwa-mul*	수화물
ball	*kong*	공
bank	*ŭn-haeng*	은행
banknote	*ŭn-haeng-kwŏn*	은행권
bar	*ba*	바
barbeque	*ba-bi-k'yu*	바비큐
battery	*bae-t'ŏ-ri*	배터리
beach	*hae-su-yok-jang*	해수욕장
beautiful	*a-rŭm-da-un*	아름다운
because	*wae-nya-ha-myŏn*	왜냐하면
bed	*ch'im-dae*	침대
bedbug	*bin-dae*	빈대
before	*jŏn-e*	전에
beggar	*kŏ-ji*	거지
begin	*shi-jak-ha-da*	시작하다
beginner	*ch'o-bu-ja*	초보자
behind	*dwi-e*	뒤에
believe	*mit-da*	믿다
below	*a-rae-e*	아래에
beside	*kyŏt-e*	곁에
best	*ka-jang jo-hŭn*	가장 좋은

better	*dŏ jo-hŭn*	더 좋은
between	*sa-i-e*	사이에
bicycle	*ja-jŏn-kŏ*	자전거
big	*k'ŭn*	큰
bill	*kye-san-sŏ*	계산서
birthday	*saeng-il*	생일
bitter	*ji-dok-han*	지독한
blind	*nun mŏn*	눈 먼
blood	*p'i*	피
body	*mom*	몸
bomb	*p'ok-t'an*	폭탄
book (n)	*ch'aek*	책
bookshop	*sŏ-jŏm*	서점
bored, I'm	*shim-shim-ham-ni-da*	심심합니다
borrow	*bil-li-da*	빌리다
May I borrow this?	*i-gŏ-sŭl bil lil su iss-sŭm-ni-kka?*	이것을 빌릴 수 있습니까?
boss	*sa-jang*	사장
both	*yang-jjo-gŭi*	양쪽의
bottle	*byŏng*	병
bottle opener	*byŏng-ma-gae-ppop-i*	병 마개뽑이
box	*sang-ja*	상차
boy	*so-nyŏn*	소년
boyfriend	*nam-ja ch'in-gu*	남자 친구
brave	*yong-gam-han*	용감한
break (v)	*bu-rŏ-ji-da*	부러지다
break (pause)	*jung-dan*	중단
breakfast	*a-ch'im shik-sa*	아침 식사
breastfeed	*mo-yu-rŭl ju-da*	모유를 주다

VOCABULARY

bribe (n)	*noe-mul*	뇌물
bribe (v)	*noe-mul-ŭl ju-da*	뇌물을 주다
bridge	*da-ri*	다리
bright	*bal-gŭn*	밝은
bring	*ka-jyŏ-o-da*	가져오다
May I bring ...?	*... ka-jyŏ ol-ga-yo?*	... 가져 올까요?
broken	*bu-sŏ-jin*	부서진
build (v)	*se-u-da*	세우다
building	*kŏn-mul*	건물
burn	*hwa-sang*	화상
bus	*bŏ-sŭ*	버스
business	*sa-ŏp*	사업
business hours	*yŏng-ŏp shi-kan*	영업 시간
busy (to be) (v)	*ba-ppŭ-da*	바쁘다
Are you busy?	*ba-ppŭ-shim-ni-kka?*	바쁩니까?
but	*kŭ-rŏ-na*	그러나
buy	*sa-da*	사다

C

café	*k'a-p'e*	카페
camera	*k'a-me-ra*	카메라
camp (n)	*k'aem-p'ŭ*	캠프
camp (v)	*k'aem-p'ŭ-ha-da*	캠프하다
can (able to)	*hal su id-da*	할 수 있다
I can't.	*hal su ŏp-da*	할 수 없다
capital (city)	*su-do*	수도
capitalism	*ja-bon-ju-ŭi*	자본주의
car	*ja-dong-ch'a*	자동차
cards (playing)	*k'a-dŭ (no-ri)*	카드(놀이)
care (n)	*jo-shim*	조심
careful	*jo-shim-sŏng id-nŭn*	조심성 있는

carry (v)	*un-ban-ha-d*	운반하다
cemetery	*myo-ji*	묘지
centre	*ka-un-de*	가운데
certain	*hwak-shil-han*	확실한
I am certain.	*hwak-shil-ham-ni-da*	확실합니다
Are you certain?	*hwak-shil-ham-ni-kka?*	확실합니까?
chance	*ki-hoe*	기회
chair	*ŭi-ja*	의자
change (v)	*ba-kku-da*	바꾸다
cheap	*san*	싼
chemist	*yak-kuk*	약국
child	*ŏ-rin-i*	어린이
chocolate	*ch'o-k'ol-rit*	초콜릿
choose	*sŏn-t'aek-ha-da*	선택하다
Christmas	*k'ŭ-ri-sŭ-ma-sŭ*	성탄절
chopsticks	*jŏt-ga-rak*	젓가락
church	*kyo-hoe*	교회
cigarettes	*dam-bae*	담배
cigarette papers	*dam-bae jong-i*	담배 종이
city	*do-shi*	도시
clean (adj)	*kkae-kkŭt-han*	깨끗한
clock	*shi-kye*	시계
close (v)	*dat-da*	닫다
close (adj)	*ka-ga-un*	가까운
clothes	*ot*	옷
coin	*dong-jŏn*	동전
cold	*ch'up-da*	춥다
come	*o-da*	오다
I am coming.	*o-go iss-sŭm-ni-da*	오고 있습니다
Are you coming?	*o-shim-ni-kka?*	오십니까?

comfortable	*p'yŏn-an-han*	편안한
communism	*kong-san-ju-ŭi*	공산주의
company (firm)	*hoe-sa*	회사
complex	*bok-jap-han*	복잡한
condom	*k'on-dom*	콘돔
Congratulations!	*ch'uk-ha!*	축하!
consulate	*yŏng-sa-gwan*	영사관
contraceptive	*p'i-im-yak*	피임약
conversation	*dae-hwa*	대화
cook (v)	*yo-ri-ha-da*	요리하다
cooperative	*hyŏp-jo-jŏ-gin*	협조적인
corner	*mo-t'ung-i*	모퉁이
corrupt	*bu-jŏng-han*	부정한
corruption	*bu-jŏng bu-p'ae*	부정 부패
cost (n)	*bi-yong*	비용
How much does it cost?	*ŏl-ma-im-ni-kka?*	얼마입니까?
count (v)	*kye-san-ha-da*	계산하다
countryside	*shi-gol*	시골
crazy	*mi-ch'in*	미친
credit card	*shin-yong k'a-dŭ*	신용 카드
cup	*k'ŏp*	컵
customs (officials)	*se-gwan*	세관
cut (v)	*kkak-da*	깎다

D

daily	*mae-il*	매일
damp	*ch'uk-ch'uk-han*	축축한
dangerous	*wi-hŏm-han*	위험한
dark	*ŏ-du-un*	어두운
date (time)	*nal-jja*	날짜

VOCABULARY

dawn	*sae-byŏk*	새벽
day	*il*	일
dead	*ju-gŭn*	죽은
deaf	*kwi-ga mŏn*	귀가 먼
death	*ju-gŭm*	죽음
decide	*kyŏl-jŏng-ha-da*	결정하다
decision	*kyŏl-jŏng*	결정
delay (n)	*yŏn-gi*	연기
delay (v)	*yŏn-gi-ha-da*	연기하다
delicious	*mat-id-nŭn*	맛있는
democracy	*min-ju-ju-ŭi*	민주주의
demonstration	*de-mo-un-dong*	데모운동
dentist	*ch'i-gwa-ŭi*	치과의
depart (v)	*ch'ul-bal-ha-da*	출발하다
departure	*ch'ul-bal*	출발
descend (v)	*nae-ryŏ-ka-da*	내려가다
destroy (v)	*p'a-goe-ha-da*	파괴하다
development	*bal-dal*	발달
dictionary	*sa-jŏn*	사전
different	*da-rŭn*	다른
difficult	*ŏ-ryŏ-un*	어려운
dinner	*jŏ-nyŏk*	저녁
direct (adj)	*ttok-ba-rŭn*	곧바로
dirty	*dŏ-rŏ-un*	더러운
disadvantage	*dan-jŏm*	단점
discount	*hal-in*	할인
discrimination	*ch'a-byŏl*	차별
do (v)	*ha-da*	하다
I can do it.	*hal su iss-sŭm-ni-da*	할 수 있습니다
Can you do it?	*hal su iss-sŭm-ni-kka?*	할 수 있습니까?

doctor	*ŭi-sa*	의사
dollar	*dal-lŏ*	달러
double	*du bae*	두 배
down	*a-rae*	아래
downstairs	*a-rae-ch'ŭng*	아래층
downtown	*shi-nae*	시내
dream (n)	*kkum*	꿈
dried	*mal-rin*	말린
drink (n)	*ma-shil kŏt*	마실 것
drink (v)	*ma-shi-da*	마시다
drinkable (water)	*shik-sŭ*	식수
driver	*un-jŏn-sa*	운전사
drunk (inebriated)	*sul-ju-jŏng-baeng-i*	술 주정뱅이
dry	*ma-rŭn*	마른
drycleaning	*se-t'ak-so*	세탁소
during	*jung-e*	중에

E

each	*kak-gak*	각각
early	*il-jjik*	일찍
earn	*bŏl-da*	벌다
earnings	*so-dŭk*	소득
Earth	*Ji-ku*	지구
earthquake	*ji-jin*	지진
Easter	*bu-hwal-jŏl*	부활절
easy	*swi-un*	쉬운
eat	*mŏk-da*	먹다
economical	*kyŏng-je-jŏ-gin*	경제적인
economy	*kyŏng-je*	경제
education	*kyo-yuk*	교육
elder	*yŏn-jang-ja*	연장자

VOCABULARY

election	*sŏn-gŏ*	선거
electricity	*jŏn-gi*	전기
elevator	*el-li-be-i-t'ŏ*	엘리베이터
embarrassment	*dang-hwang*	당황
embassy	*dae-sa-gwan*	대사관
employee	*ko-yong-in*	고용인
employer	*ko-yong-ju*	고용주
empty	*bin*	빈
end (n)	*kkŭt*	끝
English	*Yŏng-ŏ*	영어
enjoy	*jŭl-gi-da*	즐기다
enough	*ch'ung-bun-han*	충분한
enter	*dŭ-rŏ-ga-da*	들어가다
entrance	*ip-gu*	입구
equal	*ka-tŏn*	같은
evening	*jŏ-nyŏk*	저녁
event	*sa-gŏn*	사건
ever (always)	*ŏn-je-na*	언제나
every	*mo-dŭn*	모든
everybody	*nu-gu-dŭn-ji*	누구든지
everything	*mo-du*	모두
exchange (v)	*kyo-hwan-ha-da*	교환하다
exhausted	*ji-ch'in*	지친
exit	*ch'ul-gu*	출구
expensive	*bi-sa-da*	비싸다
experience (n)	*kyŏng-hŏm*	경험
export (v)	*su-ch'ul-ha-da*	수출하다
export (n)	*su-ch'ul-p'um*	수출품
explain	*sŏl-myŏng-ha-da*	설명하다
Please explain.	*sŏl-myŏng-ha-yŏ ju-ship-shi-yo*	설명하여 주십시오

F

false	*kŏ-jit-ŭi*	거짓의
family	*ka-jok*	가족
fan (electric)	*sŏn-p'ung-gi*	선풍기
far	*mŏl-li*	멀리
farm	*nong-jang*	농장
fast (quick)	*ppa-rŭn*	빠른
fat	*sal-jjin*	살찐
fault (defect)	*kyŏl-jŏm*	결점
fear	*kong-p'o*	공포
fee	*su-su-ryo*	수수료
feel	*nŭ-kki-da*	느끼다
ferry	*hwe-ri*	훼리
festival	*ch'uk-je*	축제
fever	*yŏl*	열
few	*su-ka jŏ-gŭn*	수가 적은
fight (n)	*sa-um*	싸움
film	*p'il-rŭm*	필름
find	*ch'a-ja-nae-da*	찾아내다
fine (penalty)	*bŏl-gŭm*	벌금
fire	*bul*	불
firewood	*jang-jak*	장작
first	*ch'ŏt-jjae-ŭi*	첫째의
flag	*kuk-gi*	국기
flight	*bi-haeng*	비행
flood	*hong-su*	홍수
floor	*ma-rŭt-ba-dak*	마룻바닥
fly (v)	*nal-da*	날다
follow (v)	*tta-la-ga-da*	따라가다
foreign	*oe-guk-ŭi*	외국의
forever	*yŏng-wŏn-hi*	영원히

forget	*it-da*	잊다
I forgot.	*jŏ bŏ-ryŏd-da*	잊어 버렸다
Did you forget?	*jŏ bŏ-ri-syŏss-sŭm-ni-kka?*	잊어 버리셨습니까?
forgive (v)	*yong-sŏ-ha-da*	용서하다
formal	*jŏng-shik-ŭi*	정식의
formality	*jŏng-shik*	정식
fragile	*yŏn-yak-han*	연약한
free (of charge)	*mu-ryo*	무료
free (not bound)	*ja-yu-ro-un*	자유로운
freeze	*ŏl-ŭm-i ŏl-da*	얼음이 얼다
fresh	*shin-sŏn-han*	신선한
friend	*ch'in-gu*	친구
friendly	*ch'in-jŏl-han*	친절한
from	*bu-t'ŏ*	부터
full	*ka-dŭk ch'an*	가득 찬
fun	*jang-nan*	장난
funny	*u-sŭ-un*	우스운

G

game	*ke-im*	게임
garbage	*sŭ-re-ki*	쓰레기
garden	*jŏng-wŏn*	정원
generous	*kwan-dae-han*	관대한
girl	*so-nyŏ*	소녀
girlfriend	*yŏ-ja-ch'in-gu*	여자친구
give	*ju-da*	주다
Give it to me!	*je-ge ju-se-yo!*	제게 주세요!
glass (of water)	*yu-ri-jan*	유리잔
glasses (spectacles)	*an-gyŏng*	안경

go	ka-da	가다
I am going.	ga-go iss-sŭm-ni-da	가고 있습니다
Are you going?	ka-shi-gess-sŭm-ni-kka?	가시겠습니까?
God	Ha-nŭ-nim	하느님
good	jo-hŭn	좋은
government	jŏng-bu	정부
greedy	yok-shim-ma-nŭn	욕심 많은
grow	sŏng-jang-ha-da	성장하다
guess (v)	ch'u-ch'ŭk-ha-da	추측하다
guide (n)	an-nae-ja	안내자
guide (v)	an-nae-ha-da	안내하다
guidebook	an-nae-sŏ	안내서
guilty	yu-joe-ŭi	유죄의

H

half	ban	반
handbag	son-ka-bang	손가방
handicraft	su-je-p'um	수제품
handsome	jal-saeng-gin	잘생긴
happy	haeng-bok-han	행복한
hard (not soft)	dan-dan-han	단단한
hate (v)	mi-wŏ-ha-da	미워하다
I hate ...	... mi-wŏ-ha-da	... 미워하다
have	ka-ji-da	가지다
I have ...	... ka-ji-go iss-sŭm-ni-da	... 가지고 있습니다
Do you have ...?	... ka-ji-go iss-sŭm-ni-kka?	... 가지고 있습니까?
health	kŏn-gang	건강
hear	dŭt-da	듣다

heat	*yŏl*	열
heater	*nan-bang jang-ch'i*	난방 장치
heavy	*mu-gŏ-un*	무거운
Hello.	*yŏ-bo-se-yo*	여보세요
help (v)	*dop-da*	돕다
Help me!	*do-wa ju-se-yo!*	도와 주세요!
here	*yŏ-gi*	여기
high	*nop-ŭn*	높은
hire (v)	*bil-li-da*	빌리다
I'd like to hire it.	*kŭ-gŏ-sŭl bil-li-go ship-sŭm-ni-da*	그것을 빌리고 싶습니다
hitchhike	*hi-ch'i-ha-i-k'ŭ*	히치하이크
holiday	*hyu-ga*	휴가
home	*ka-jŏng*	가정
homesick	*hyang-su-byŏng*	향수병
homosexual	*dong-sŏng-ae-in*	동성애인
honest	*jŏng-jik-han*	정직한
hope (n)	*hŭi-mang*	희망
hope (v)	*ba-ra-da*	바라다
I hope so.	*kŭ-rŏ-ke dwoe-gi-rŭl ba-ram-ni-da*	그렇게 되기를 바랍니다
hospitality	*chi'n-jŏl-hi jŏp-dae-ham*	친절히 접대함
hot	*ttŭ-gŏ-un*	뜨거운
hotel	*ho-t'el*	호텔
house	*jip*	집
housework	*ka-sa*	가사
how	*ŏ-ttŏ-ke*	어떻게
How much is it?	*ŏl-ma-im-ni-kka?*	얼마입니까?
How do I get to ...?	*ŏ-ttŏ-ke kam-ni-kka ...?*	... 어떻게 갑니

hug (v)	*kkyŏ-an-da*	껴안다
human	*in-gan*	인간
hungry	*bae-go-p'ŭn*	배고픈
I am hungry.	*bae-ga ko-p'ŭm-ni-da.*	배다 고픕니다
Are you hungry?	*bae-ga ko-p'ŭ-shim-ni-kka?*	배가 고프십니까?
hurry (v)	*sŏ-du-rŭ-da*	서두르다
I'm in a hurry.	*kŭ-pae-yo*	급해요
hurt	*a-pŭm*	아픔

I

ice	*ŏl-ŭm*	얼음
idea	*a-i-di-ŏ*	아이디어
identification	*shin-bun-jŭng*	신분증
if	*man-yak*	만약
ill	*byŏng-dŭn*	병든
illegal	*bul-bŏp-ŭi*	불법의
imagination	*sang-sang*	상상
immediately	*dang-jang*	당장
imitation	*mo-bang*	모방
import (n)	*su-ip*	수입
import (v)	*su-ip-ha-da*	수입하다
impossible	*bul-ga-nŭng-han*	불가능한
imprison	*kam-o-ge nŏ-t'a*	감옥에 넣다
imprisonment	*kam-gŭm*	감금
in	*an-e*	안에
incident	*ja-gŭn sa-gŏn*	작은 사건
include	*p'o-ham-ha-da*	포함하다
inconvenient	*bul-p'yŏn-han*	불편한
individual	*kae-in*	개인

industry	*san-ŏp*	산업
informal	*bi-gong-shik-ŭi*	비공식의
information	*jŏng-bo*	정보
inside	*an-jjok*	안쪽
insurance	*bo-hŏm*	보험
insure	*bo-hŏm-e dŭl-da*	보험에 들다
It's insured.	*bo-hŏm-e dŭ-rŏ*	보험에 들어
	iss-sŭm-ni-da	있습니다
intelligent	*ch'ong-myŏng-han*	총명한
interesting	*hŭng-mi*	흥미
international	*kuk-je-jŏ-gin*	국제적인
invite (v)	*ch'o-dae-ha-da*	초대하다

J

jail	*kam-ok*	감옥
jazz	*jae-jŭ*	재즈
job	*jik-ŏp*	직업
joke (n)	*nong-dam*	농담
I'm joking.	*nong-dam-im-ni-da*	농담입니다
justice	*jŏng-ŭi*	정의

K

key	*yŏl-soe*	열쇠
kill	*juk-i-da*	죽이다
kind (adj)	*ch'in-jŏl-han*	친절한
kiss (n)	*k'i-sŭ*	키스
know	*al-da*	알다
I know.	*al-gess-sŭm-ni-da*	알겠습니다
I don't know.	*mo-rŭ-gess-sŭm-ni-da*	모르겠습니다
Korea	*Han-guk*	한국

Korean	*Han-guk-sa-ram*	한국사람

L

lake	*ho-su*	호수
land	*yuk-ji*	육지
language	*ŏn-ŏ*	언어
last (adj)	*ma-ji-mak-ŭi*	마지막의
late	*nŭ-jŭn*	늦은
later	*na-jung-e*	나중에
laugh (v)	*ut-da*	웃다
laundry	*se-t'ak-so*	세탁소
law	*bŏp*	법
lawyer	*bŏm-ryul-ga*	법률가
lazy	*ke-ŭ-rŭn*	게으른
learn	*bae-u-da*	배우다
leave	*ttŏ-na-da*	떠나다
left (opposite of right)	*oen-jjok*	왼쪽
legal	*hap-bŏp-jŏ-gin*	합법적인
less	*bo-da jŏ-gŭn*	보다 적은
letter	*p'yŏn-ji*	편지
library	*do-sŏ-kwan*	도서관
lie (recline)	*nup-da*	눕다
life	*saeng-myŏng*	생명
lift (elevator)	*el-li-be-i-t'ŏ*	엘리베이터
light (opposite of heavy)	*ka-byŏ-un*	가벼운
like	*jo-a-ha-da*	좋아하다
I like ...	*... jo-a-ham-ni-da*	... 좋아합니다
Do you like ...?	*... jo-a-ha-shim-ni-kka?*	... 좋아하십니까?

listen	*dŭt-da*	듣다
little	*ja-gŭn*	작은
live (v)	*sal-da*	살다
lock (n)	*ja-mul-soe*	자물쇠
look for	*ch'at-da*	찾다
long	*kin*	긴
lose	*ji-da*	지다
lost	*i-rŭn*	잃은
I am lost.	*i-rŏ bŏ-ryŏss-sŭm-ni-da*	잃어 버렸습니다
loud	*so-ri-ga k'ŭn*	소리가 큰
love (n)	*sa-rang*	사랑
love (v)	*sa-rang-ha-da*	사랑하다
luck	*haeng-un*	행운
lucky	*haeng-un-ŭi*	행운의
lunch	*jŏm-shim*	점심

M

machine	*ki-gye*	기계
mad (crazy)	*mi-ch'in*	미친
magazine	*jap-ji*	잡지
majority	*dae-da-su*	대다수
make	*man-dŭl-da*	만들다
What is it made of?	*mu-ŏ-sŭ-ro man-dŭ-rŏss-sŭm-ni-kka?*	무엇으로 만들었습니까?
manager	*ji-bae-in*	지배인
many	*su-ga man-ŭn*	수가 많은
map	*ji-do*	지도
market	*shi-jang*	시장
marriage	*kyŏl-hon*	결혼
marry	*kyŏl-hon-ha-da*	결혼하다

VOCABULARY

matches	*sŏng-nyang*	성냥
maybe	*a-ma*	아마
medicine	*yak*	약
meet	*man-na-da*	만나다
Meet me at ...	*... -e-sŏ man-nap-shi-da*	...에서 만납시다
mend	*su-sŏn-ha-da*	수선하다
menu	*me-nyu*	메뉴
message	*me-shi-ji*	메시지
mind (n)	*saeng-gak*	생각
minute (time)	*bun*	분
mistake	*jal-mot*	잘못
miss (v)	*no-ch'i-da*	놓치다
mix (v)	*sŏk-da*	섞다
modern	*hyŏn-dae-shik*	현대식
money	*don*	돈
more	*dŏ*	더
morning	*a-ch'im*	아침
move	*um-jik-i-da*	움직이다
movie	*yŏng-hwa*	영화
museum	*bak-mul-gwan*	박물관
music	*ŭm-ak*	음악

N

name	*i-rŭm*	이름
My name is ...	*je i-rŭm-ŭn ... im-ni-da*	제 이름은 ...입니다
nationality	*kuk-jŏk*	국적
nature	*ja-yŏn*	자연
near	*ka-ga-i*	가까이
necessary	*p'il-yo-han*	필요한

need (v)	*p'il-yo-ha-da*	필요하다
never	*jŏl-dae-ro*	절대로
new	*sae-ro-un*	새로운
news	*nyu-sŭ*	뉴스
newspaper	*shin-mun*	신문
next	*da-ŭm*	다음
night	*bam*	밤
no	*a-ni-yo*	아니오
noise	*so-ŭm*	소음
noisy	*shi-kkŭ-rŏ-un*	시끄러운
now	*ji-gŭm*	지금
number	*bŏn-ho*	번호

O

obvious	*myŏng-baek-han*	명백한
occupation	*jik-ŏp*	직업
ocean	*dae-yang*	대양
offend (v)	*choe-rŭl bŏm-ha-da*	죄를 범하다
offer (v)	*je-gong-ha-da*	제공하다
office	*sa-mu-shil*	사무실
often	*hŭn-hi*	흔히
oil	*ki-rŭm*	기름
ointment	*yŏn-go*	연고
old	*nŭl-gŭn*	늙은
on	*wi-e*	위에
once	*han bŏn*	한 번
one	*ha-na*	하나
only	*da-man*	다만
open (v)	*yŏl-da*	열다
opinion	*ŭi-gyŏn*	의견
opportunity	*ki-hoe*	기회

opposite	*ban-dae-p'yŏn*	반대편
or	*tto-nŭn*	또는
order (n)	*ju-mun*	주문
ordinary	*bo-t'ong*	보통
organisation	*jo-jik*	조직
original	*wŏn-bon*	원본
other	*da-rŭn*	다른
out	*bak-e*	밖에
outside	*ba-gat-jjok*	바깥쪽
over	*wi-jjok-e*	위쪽에
overnight	*bam-sae*	밤새
overseas	*hae-oe*	해외
owe	*so-yu-ha-da*	소유하다
I owe you ...	*je-ga ... dang-shin-e-ge dŭ-ryŏ ya ham-ni-da*	제가 ... 당신에게 드려야 합니다
You owe me ...	*dang-shin-i ... je-ge ju-syŏ-ya ham-ni-da*	당신이 ... 제게 주셔야 합니다
owner	*ju-in*	주인

P

package	*kku-rŏ-mi*	꾸러미
packet	*han mu-gŭm*	한 묶음
padlock	*ja-mul-soe*	자물쇠
pain	*ko-t'ong*	고통
painful	*a-p'ŭn*	아픈
pair	*sang*	쌍
paper	*jong-i*	종이
park (n)	*kong-wŏn*	공원
participate (v)	*ch'am-yŏ-ha-da*	참여하다
participation	*ch'am-ga*	참가

particular	*t'ŭk-hi*	특히
party	*p'a-t'i*	파티
passenger	*sŭng-gaek*	승객
passport	*yŏ-gwŏn*	여권
past (n)	*kwa-gŏ*	과거
pay (v)	*ji-bul-ha-da*	지불하다
peace	*p'yŏng-hwa*	평화
perfect (adj)	*wan-jŏn-han*	완전한
permission	*hŏ-ga*	허가
permit (v)	*hŏ-rak-ha-da*	허락하다
persecution	*bak-hae*	박해
person	*sa-ram*	사람
personal	*kae-in-jŏk-in*	개인적인
personality	*sŏng-kyŏk*	성격
perspire	*ttam-ŭl hŭl-ri-da*	땀을 흘리다
pharmacy	*yak-kuk*	약국
photograph (n)	*sa-jin*	사진
photograph (v)	*sa-jin-ŭl jjik-da*	사진을 찍다
May I take photographs?	*sa-jn jom jjik-ŏ-do doem-ni-kka?*	사진 좀 찍어도 됩니까?
pill	*al-yak*	알약
place	*jang-so*	장소
play (v)	*nol-da*	놀다
police	*kŏng-ch'al*	경찰
politics	*jŏng-ch'i*	정치
pool (swimming)	*su-yŏng-jang*	수영장
poor	*ka-nan*	가난
positive	*kŭng-jŏng-jŏk-in*	긍정적인
postbox	*u-ch'e-t'ong*	우체통
post office	*u-ch'e-guk*	우체국
poverty	*bin-gon*	빈곤

power	*him*	힘
prayer	*ki-do*	기도
prefer	*dŏ jo-a-ha-da*	더 좋아하다
I prefer ...	*... dŏ jo-a-ha-da*	... 더 좋아합니다
What do you prefer?	*mu-ŏ-sŭl dŏ jo-a-ham-ni-kka?*	무엇을 더 좋아합니까?
pregnant	*im-shin-han*	임신한
prepare	*jun-bi-ha-da*	준비하다
present (time)	*hyŏn-jae*	현재
present (gift)	*sŏn-mul*	선물
president	*dae-t'ong-ryŏng*	대통령
pretty	*ye-ppŭn*	예쁜
prevent	*ye-bang-ha-da*	예방하다
price	*ka-gyŏk*	가격
priest	*sŏng jik-ja*	성직자
prison	*kam-ok*	감옥
prisoner	*joe-su*	죄수
private	*kae-in-jŏ-gin*	개인적인
probably	*a-ma*	아마
problem	*mun-je*	문제
procession	*haeng-jin*	행진
produce (v)	*saeng-san-ha-da*	생산하다
professional	*jŏn-mun-ga*	전문가
profit	*i-ik*	이익
promise (n)	*yak-sok*	약속
property	*jae-san*	재산
prostitute	*ch'ang-nyŏ*	창녀
protect	*bo-ho-ha-da*	보호하다
protest (n)	*hang-ŭi*	항의
public	*kong-jung*	공중
pull	*dang-gi-da*	당기다

punish	*bŏl-ha-da*	벌하다
push (v)	*mil-da*	밀다
put (v)	*no-da*	놓다

Q

quality	*p'um-jil*	품질
quantity	*bun-ryang*	분량
question	*jil-mun*	질문
quick	*ppa-rŭn*	빠른
quiet	*jo-yong-han*	조용한

R

race (of people)	*in-jong*	인종
race (contest)	*kyŏng-ju*	경주
racism	*in-jong-jŏk ch'a-byŏl*	인종적 차별
radio	*ra-di-o*	라디오
rain	*bi*	비
rape (n)	*kang-gan*	강간
rape (v)	*kang-gan-ha-da*	강간하다
rare	*dŭ-mun*	드문
read (v)	*il-da*	읽다
ready	*jun-bi-doen*	준비된
reason	*i-yu*	이유
receipt	*yŏng-su-jŭng*	영수증
receive (v)	*bat-da*	받다
recently	*ch'oe-gŭn-e*	최근에
recommend	*ch'u-ch'ŏn-ha-da*	추천하다
Can you recommend a ...?	*... ch'u-ch'ŏn-hae ju-shi-gess-sŭm-ni-kka?*	... 추천해 주시겠습니까?

recording	*no-gŭm*	녹음
refuse (v)	*kŏ-jŏl-ha-da*	거절하다
region	*ji-yŏk*	지역
regulation	*kyu-jŏng*	규정
relationship	*kwan-gye*	관계
relax	*him-ŭl ppae-da*	힘을 빼다
religion	*jong-gyo*	종교
remember	*ki-ŏk-ha-da*	기억하다
remote	*mŏn*	먼
rent (n)	*jip-se*	집세
rent (v)	*im-dae-ha-da*	임대하다
repair (v)	*su-sŏn-ha-da*	수선하다
repeat	*ban-bok-ha-da*	반복하다
Could you repeat that, please?	*da-shi bŏn-bok-hae ju-ship-shi-yo?*	다시 반복해 주십시오?
representative	*dae-p'yo-ja*	대표자
republic	*kong-hwa-guk*	공화국
require	*yo-gu-ha-da*	요구하다
reservation	*ye-yak*	예약
respect (n)	*jon-gyŏng*	존경
responsibility	*ch'ae-gim*	책임
rest (n)	*hyu-shik*	휴식
restaurant	*re-sŭ-t'o-rang*	레스토랑
revolution	*hyŏk-myŏng*	혁명
rich	*bu-ja*	부자
right (opposite of left)	*o-rŭn-jjok*	오른쪽
right, I'm	*je-ga ma-ja-ssŏ-yo*	제가 맞았어요
risk	*wi-hŏm*	위험
road	*kil*	길
robber	*do-duk*	도둑

robbery	*do-duk-jil*	도둑질
roof	*ji-bung*	지붕
room	*bang*	방
rope	*bat-jul*	밧줄
round	*dung-gŭn*	동근
rubbish	*sŭ-re-gi*	쓰레기
ruins	*p'ye-hŏ*	폐허
rule	*kyu-ch'ik*	규칙
run (v)	*dal-li-da*	달리다

S

sad	*sŭl-p'ŭn*	슬픈
safe (adj)	*an-jŏn-han*	안전한
safety	*an-jŏn*	안전
same	*kat-ŭn*	같은
satisfaction	*man-chok*	만족
save	*ku-ha-da*	구하다
say	*mal-ha-da*	말하다
Can you say that again, please?	*da-shi mal-sŭm-hae ju-shi-gess-sŭm-ni-kka?*	다시 말씀해 주시겠습니까?
school	*hak-gyo*	학교
seasick	*bae-mŏl-mi*	뱃멀미
secret	*bi-mil*	비밀
see	*bo-da*	보다
I see. (understand)	*al-gess-sŭm-ni-da*	알겠습니다
I see. (it)	*bo-im-ni-da*	보입니다
selfish	*i-gi-jŏ-gin*	이기적인
sell	*p'al-da*	팔다
send	*bo-nae-da*	보내다
separate (adj)	*kal-la-jin*	갈라진

separate (v)	*bun-ri-ha-da*	분리하다
several	*su-gae-ŭi*	수개의
sew	*ba-nŭ-jil-ha-da*	바느질하다
shade (n)	*kŭ-nŭl*	그늘
shampoo	*syam-p'u*	샴푸
share (v)	*bun-bae-ha-da*	분배하다
ship	*bae*	배
shop (n)	*sang-jŏm*	상점
short (time)	*jjal-bŭn*	짧은
short (height)	*k'i-ga ja-gŭn*	키가 작은
shortage	*bu-jok*	부족
shout (v)	*oe-ch'i-da*	외치다
show (v)	*bo-i-da*	보이다
Show me.	*bo-yŏ ju-ship-shi-yo*	보여 주십시오
shy	*su-jup-ŭn*	수줍은
sickness	*byŏng*	병
sign	*shin-ho*	신호
silence	*ch'im-muk*	침묵
similar	*bi-sŭt-han*	비슷한
simple	*kan-dan-han*	간단한
single (unique)	*dan ha-na-ŭi*	단 하나의
single (unmarried)	*dok-shin*	독신
sit	*an-da*	앉다

I want to sit down.	*ja-ri-e an-go*	자리에 앉고
	ship-sŭm-ni-da	싶습니다
situation	*wi-ch'i*	위치
size	*k'ŭ-gi*	크기
sleep (v)	*ja-da*	자다
slow	*nŭ-rin*	느린
slowly	*nŭ-ri-ge*	느리게

small	*ja-gŭn*	작은
smell (n)	*naem-sae*	냄새
smile (n)	*mi-so*	미소
socialism	*sa-hwoe-ju-ŭi*	사회주의
somebody	*ŏ-ttŏn sa-ram*	어떤 사람
something	*ŏ-ttŏn kot*	어떤 것
sometimes	*ka-kkŭm*	가끔
song	*no-rae*	노래
soon	*kot*	곧
sorry, I'm	*mi-an-ham-ni-da*	미안합니다
souvenir	*ki-nyŏm-p'um*	기념품
speak (v)	*mal-ha-da*	말하다
special	*t'ŭk-byŏl-han*	특별한
sport	*un-dong*	운동
spring (season)	*bom*	봄
standard (n)	*p'yo-jun*	표준
start (v)	*shi-jak-ha-da*	시작하다
station	*jŏng-ryu-jang*	정류장
stay (v)	*mŏ-mul-da*	머물다
steal	*hum-ch'i-da*	훔치다
stop (v)	*mŏm-ch'u-da*	멈추다
Stop it!	*jŏng-ji!*	중지!
story (tale)	*i-ya-ki*	이야기
straight	*ttok-ba-ro*	똑바로
strange	*i-sang-han*	이상한
stranger	*nat-sŏn sa-ram*	낯선 사람
street	*kil*	길
strength	*him*	힘
strong	*him-sen*	힘센
stupid	*ŏ-ri-sŏ-gŭn*	어리석은
sudden	*kap-jak-sŭ-rŏ-un*	갑작스러운

VOCABULARY

summer	yŏ-rŭm	여름
sun	t'ae-yang	태양
sure	hwak-shil-han	확실한
Are you sure?	hwak-shil-ham-ni-kka?	확실합니까?
survive	sal-a-nam-da	살아남다
sweet	dan-mat	단맛

T

take (v)	ka-ji-go ka da	가지고 가다
take off	bŏt-da	벗다
talk (v)	mal-ha-da	말하다
tall	k'i-ga k'ŭn	키가 큰
tasty	mat-id-nŭn	맛있는
tax	se-gŭm	세금
taxi	t'aek-shi	택시
teach (v)	ka-rŭ-ch'i-da	가르치다
telegram	jŏn-bo	전보
telephone (n)	jŏn-hwa	전화
May I use the telephone?	jŏn-hwa-rŭl sa-yong-hae-do doep-ni-kka?	전화를 사용해도 됩니까?
telephone (v)	jŏn-hwa-ha-da	전화하다
television	t'el-le-bi-jon	텔레비전
temperature	ch'e-on	체온
tent	t'en-t'ŭ	텐트
Thank you.	kam-sa-ham-ni-da	감사합니다
that	jŏ-gŏt	저것
there	kŏ-gi	거기
thick	du-gŏ-un	두꺼운
thief	do-duk	도둑

VOCABULARY

thin	*yal-bŭn*	얇은
think	*saeng-gak-ha-da*	생각하다
thirsty	*mok-ma-rŭn*	목마른
this	*i-gŏt*	이것
thought	*saeng-gak*	생각
ticket	*p'yo*	표
tight	*kkok gi-nŭn*	꼭 끼는
time	*shi-gan*	시간
What time is it?	*myŏt shi im-ni-kka?*	몇 시 입니까?
tip (gratuity)	*t'ip*	팁
tired, I'm	*p'i-gon-ham-ni-da*	피곤합니다
together	*ham-kke*	함께
toilet	*hwa-jang-shil*	화장실
toilet paper	*hwa-jang-ji*	화장지
tonight	*o-nŭl-bam*	오늘밤
too	*yŏk-shi*	역시
toothache	*ch'i-t'ong*	치통
I have a toothache.	*i-ga a-p'ŭm-ni-da*	이가 아픕니다
touch (v)	*man-ji-da*	만지다
tour	*kwan-gwang*	관광
tourist	*kwan-gwang-gaek*	관광객
toward	*hyang-ha-yŏ*	향하여
track	*ja-gŭn kil*	작은 길
train	*ki-ch'a*	기차
transit (in)	*t'ong-haeng*	통행
translate	*bŏn-yŏk-ha-da*	번역하다
trash	*sŭ-re-gi*	쓰레기
trip	*yŏ-haeng*	여행
true	*jin-shil*	진실
trust	*shin-im*	신임
try	*shi-do-ha-da*	시도하다

U

ugly	*mip-da*	밉다
umbrella	*u-san*	우산
uncomfortable	*bul-p'yŏn-han*	불편한
under	*mit-e*	밑에
understand	*i-hae-ha-da*	이해하다
I don't understand.	*mo-rŭ-gess-sŭm-ni-da*	모르겠습니다
unemployed	*shil-jik-han*	실직한
university	*dae-hak*	대학
unsafe	*wi-hŏm-han*	위험한
until	*kka-ji*	까지
up	*wi-e*	위에
upstairs	*wi-ch'ŭng*	위층
use (v)	*sa-yong-ha-da*	사용하다
useful	*yu-yong-han*	유용한

V

vacant	*bin*	빈
vacation	*hyu-ga*	휴가
vaccination	*ye-bang-jŏp-jong*	예방접종
valuables	*kwi-jung-p'um*	귀중품
value (n)	*ka-ch'i*	가치
very	*mae-u*	매우
view (n)	*kyŏng-ch'i*	경치
village	*ma-ŭl*	마을
visit (v)	*bang-mun-ha-da*	방문하다
voice	*mok-so-ri*	목소리
vomit (v)	*t'o-ha-da*	토하다
vote (v)	*t'u-p'yo-ha-da*	투표하다

W

wait	*ki-da-ri-da*	기다리다
Wait a moment.	*jam-gan-man ki-da-ri-ship-shi-yo*	잠깐만 기다리십시오
waiter	*we-i-t'ŏ*	웨이터
walk (n)	*bo-haeng*	보행
wall	*byŏk*	벽
want	*wŏn-ha-da*	원하다
I want ...	*... wŏn-ham-ni-da*	... 원합니다
Do you want ...?	*... wŏn-ha-shim-ni-kka?*	... 원하십니까?
war	*jŏn-jaeng*	전쟁
warm	*tta-dŭt-han*	따뜻한
warning	*kyŏng-go*	경고
wash (oneself)	*sit-da*	씻다
watch (v)	*ji-k'yŏ-bo-da*	지켜보다
water	*mul*	물
way	*bang-hyang*	방향
Which way?	*ŏ-nŭ bang-hyang?*	어느 방향?
weak	*yak-han*	약한
wealth	*jae-san*	재산
wealthy	*p'ung-bu-han*	풍부한
wear	*ip-go id-da*	입고 있다
weather	*nal-shi*	날씨
wedding	*kyŏl-hon-shik*	결혼식
weight	*mu-ge*	무게
welcome	*hwan-yŏng*	환영
wet	*jŏ-jŭn*	젖은
what	*mu-ŏt*	무엇
What is that?	*jŏ-gŏ-shi mu-ŏ-shim-ni-kka?*	저것이 무엇입니까?

VOCABULARY

What does this mean?	*i-ge mu-sŭn ttŭt-im-ni-kka?*	이게 무슨 뜻입니까?
when	*ŏn-je*	언제
When is the next ...?	*da-ŭm ... ŏn-je iss-sŭm-ni-kka?*	다음... 언제 있습니까?
where	*ŏ-di*	어디
Where is ...?	*... ŏ-di-e iss-sŭm-ni-kka?*	... 어디에 있습니까?
which	*ŏ-nŭ*	어느
Which one?	*ŏ-nŭ gŏt im-ni-kka?*	어느 것 입니까?
who	*nu-gu*	누구
Who are you?	*nu-gu i-shim-ni-kka?*	누구이십니까?
Who do I ask?	*nu-gu-rŭl bu-t'ak-hae-ya ham-ni-kka?*	누구를 부탁해야 합니까?
whole	*jŏn-bu*	전부
wide	*nŏl-da*	넓다
win	*i-gi-da*	이기다
wise	*hyŏn-myŏng-ha-da*	현명하다
within	*..an-e*	...안에
without	*...ŏp-shi*	...없이
wonderful	*hul-ryung-han*	훌륭한
work (n)	*jik-ŏp*	직업
work (v)	*il-ha-da*	일하다
world	*se-kye*	세계
write	*sŭ-da*	쓰다
wrong	*na-ppŭn*	나쁜

Y

year	*nyŏn*	년
yellow	*no-rang*	노랑
yes	*ne/ye*	네/예

VOCABULARY

yesterday	*ŏ-je*	어제
yet	*a-jik*	아직
young	*jŏl-mŭn*	젊은
youth	*jŏl-mŭm*	젊음

Z

zone	*ji-yŏk*	지역
zoo	*dong-mul-wŏn*	동물원

Emergencies

It's an emergency!
ŭng-gŭp-i-ye-yo!
응급이예요!

There's been an accident!
sa-go nass-sŭm-ni-da!
사고 났습니다!

Call a doctor!
ŭi-sa bu-rŭ-se-yo!
의사 부르세요!

Call an ambulance!
ku-gŭp-ch'a bu-rŭ-se-yo!
구급차 부르세요!

I've been raped.
kang-gan dang-haess-ŏ-yo
강간 당했어요

I've been robbed!
do-duk ma-jass-ŏ-yo!
도둑 맞았어요!

Call the police!
kyŏng-ch'a-rŭl bul-lŏ ju-se-yo!
경찰을 불러 주세요!

I'll get the police!
kyŏng-ch'al bu-rŭ-gess-ŏ-yo!
경찰 부르겠어요!

Help!	*do-wa ju-se-yo!*	도와 주세요!
Stop!	*jŏng-ji!*	정지!
Go away!	*na-go-yo!/bi-k'yŏ-yo*	나가요/비켜요!
Watch out!	*Jo-shim-hae!*	조심해!
Thief!	*Do-duk-i-ya!*	도둑이야!
Fire!	*bul-i-ya!*	불이야!

My ... was stolen.	*... do-duk ma-jass-ŏ-yo*	... 도둑 맞았어요

I've lost my ...	... il-ŏ-bŏ-ryŏss- sŭm-ni-da	... 잃어버렸습니다
bags	*ka-bang*	가방
camera	*k'a-me-ra*	카메라
money	*don*	돈
passport	*yŏ-gwŏn*	여권
travellers' cheques	*yŏ-haeng-ja su-p'yo*	여행자 수표

I am ill.
a-p'ŭm-ni-da　　　　　　　　　아픕니다

I am lost.
kil-ŭl il-ŏss-sŭm-ni-da　　　　길을 잃었습니다

Where is the police station?
kyŏng-ch'al-sŏ-ga ŏ-di-e iss-　　경찰서가 어디에 있습니까?
sŭm-ni-kka?

Could you help me please?
jom do-wa ju-ship-shi-yo　　　　좀 도와 주십시오

Where are the toilets?
hwa-jang-shil-i ŏ-di-e iss-　　　화장실이 어디에 있습니까?
sŭm-ni-kka?

Could I please use the telephone?
jŏn-hwa-rŭl sa-yong-hae-do　　　전화를 사용해도 되겠습니까?
doe-gess-sŭm-ni-kka?

I wish to contact my
(embassy)/(consulate).
u-ri na-ra (dae-sa-　　　　　　우리 나라 (대사관)/(영사관)에
gwan)/(yŏng-sa-gwan) e yŏn-　　연락하고 싶습니다
rak-ha-go ship-sŭm-ni-da

I speak English.
yŏng-ŏ ham-ni-da　　　　　　　영어 합니다

I have medical insurance.
*ŭi-ryo-bo-hŏm-e dŭl-ŏ-iss-
sŭm-ni-da*

의료보험에 들어있습니다

I understand.
al-gess-sŭm-ni-da

알겠습니다

I don't understand.
mo-rŭ-gess-sŭm-ni-da

모르겠습니다

I didn't realise I was doing
anything wrong.
*jal-mot-in jul mo-rŭ-go haess-
sŭm-ni-da*

잘못인 줄 모르고 했습니다

I didn't do it.
je-ga ha-ji an-hass-sŭm-ni-da

제가 하지 않았습니다

I'm sorry.
mi-an-ham-ni-da

미안합니다

Contact number (next of kin) ...
*je bo-ho-ja yŏn-rak-bŏn-
ho-nŭn ...*

제 보호자 연락번호는...

My contact phone no. is ...
*je yŏn-rak-jŏn-hwa-bŏn-
ho-nŭn ...*

제 연락전화번호는 ...

My blood group is (A, B, O, AB)
positive/negative.
*je hyŏl-aek-hyŏng-ŭn (A, B, O,
AB) ŭm-sŏng/yang-sŏng-im-
ni-da*

제 혈액형은 (A, B, O, AB)
음성/양성입니다

My name is ...
je i-rŭm-ŭn ...

제 이름은 ...

I'm staying at ...
...-e mŏ-mul-go iss-sŭm-ni-da

... 에 머물고 있습니다

Index

LONELY PLANET PHRASEBOOKS

Complete your travel expeence with a Lonely Planet phrasebook. Developed for the independent traveller, the phrasebooks enable you to communicate confidently in any practical situation – and get to know the local people and their culture.

Skipping lengthy details on where to get your drycleaning ironed, information in the phrasebooks covers bargaining, customs and protocol, how to address people and introduce yourself, explanations of local ways of telling the time, dealing with bureaucracy and bargaining, plus plenty of ways to share your interests and learn from locals.

Arabic (Egyptian)
Arabic (Moroccan)
Australian
*Introduction to Australian English,
Aboriginal and Torres Strait languages.*
Baltic States
*Covers Estonian, Latvian and
Lithuanian.*
Bengali
Brazilian
Burmese
Cantonese
Central Asia
Central Europe
*Covers Czech, French, German,
Hungarian, Italian and Slovak.*
Eastern Europe
*Covers Bulgarian, Czech, Hungarian,
Polish, Romanian and Slovak.*
Ethiopian (Amharic)
Fijian
French
German
Greek
Hindi/Urdu
Indonesian
Italian
Japanese
Korean
Lao
Malay
Mandarin
Mongolian
Mediterranean Europe
*Covers Albanian, Greek, Italian,
Macedonian, Maltese, Serbian &
Croatian and Slovene.*

Nepali
Papua New Guinea (Pidgin)
Pilipino
Quechua
Russian
Scandinavian Europe
*Covers Danish, Finnish, Icelandic
Norwegian and Swedish.*
South-East Asia
*Covers Burmese, Indonesian, Khmer,
Lao, Malay, Tagalog (Pilipino), Thai and
Vietnamese.*
Spanish (Castilian)
*Also includes Catalan, Galician and
Basque*
Spanish (Latin American)
Sri Lanka
Swahili
Thai
Thai Hill Tribes
Tibetan
Turkish
Ukrainian
USA
*Introduction to US English,
Vernacular Talk, Native American
languages and Hawaiian.*
Vietnamese
Western Europe
*Useful words and phrases in Basque,
Catalan, Dutch, French, German, Greek,
Irish, Italian, Portuguese, Scottish
Gaelic, Spanish (Castilian) and Welsh..*

PLANET TALK
Lonely Planet's FREE quarterly newsletter

Every issue is packed with up-to-date travel news
and advice including:

* a letter from Lonely Planet co-founders Tony and
  Maureen Wheeler
* go behind the scenes on the road with a Lonely
  Planet author
* feature article on an important and topical travel
  issue
* a selection of recent letters from travellers
* details on forthcoming Lonely Planet promotions
* complete list of Lonely Planet products

PLANET TALK

Slovenia:
River Deep, Mountain High

To join our mailing list contact any Lonely Planet office.
